PRAISE FOR *IRON GODDESS*

"*Iron Goddess of Mercy* is a work ~~~~ ......, ver, activist, historian or spiritual seeker could possibly fail to fall to their knees before Lai's Iron Goddess. These are the words of a master."
—**KAI CHENG THOM**, author of *a place called No Homeland*

"Dear Reader, I'm always impressed by the power of Lai's imagination to dislocate us from reality in order to reattach us more meaningfully. In this intense, sustained long poem, Lai finds a form for everything we don't want to talk about but must."
—**IAN WILLIAMS**, author of *Personals*

"Lai allows a tumble of history to seethe through *Iron Goddess of Mercy*. A full banquet of poetic synthesis; a very satisfying poetry collection."
—**JOANNE ARNOTT**, author of *A Night for the Lady* and *Halfling Spring: an internet romance*

"In *Iron Goddess of Mercy*, Lai is breaking her way through language pileups, hooking syllables onto syntax, looping modernity over history over time. This is a tale of renewal."
—**SINA QUEYRAS**, author of *My Ariel*

"Lai's 'poethic' vision thrives by a poetry of grand imagination and sonic depth. Here is mourning and celebration as Lai deals hard-won blows to the limiting strictness of reason. Here we emerge with better names for common things in their hypnotic globe of urgent transformation."
—**CANISIA LUBRIN**, author of *The Dyzgraphxst* and *Voodoo Hypothesis*

"Dear Reader, I don't think I've ever experienced the intensity of an epistolary 'voice' performed with such impact as this Iron Goddess jamming through the syllables of an explosive imagination."
—**FRED WAH**, author of *Music at the Heart of Thinking*

IRON GODDESS OF MERCY

A POEM

LARISSA LAI

ARSENAL PULP PRESS
VANCOUVER

IRON GODDESS OF MERCY
Copyright © 2021 by Larissa Lai

ARSENAL PULP PRESS
Suite 202 – 211 East Georgia St.
Vancouver, BC V6A 1Z6
Canada
arsenalpulp.com

The publisher gratefully acknowledges the support of the Canada Council for the Arts and the British Columbia Arts Council for its publishing program, and the Government of Canada, and the Government of British Columbia (through the Book Publishing Tax Credit Program), for its publishing activities.

Arsenal Pulp Press acknowledges the xʷməθkʷəy̓əm (Musqueam), Sḵwx̱wú7mesh (Squamish) and səlilwətaʔɬ (Tsleil-Waututh) Nations, custodians of the traditional, ancestral and unceded territories where our office is located. We pay respect to their histories, traditions and continuous living cultures and commit to accountability, respectful relations and friendship.

"She Had Some Horses." Copyright © 1983 by Joy Harjo, from SHE HAD SOME HORSES by Joy Harjo. Used by permission of W. W. Norton & Company, Inc.
"Five Poems of Resurrection." Copyright © 1997 by Roy K. Kiyooka, from PACIFIC WINDOWS: COLLECTED POEMS OF ROY K. KIYOOKA by Roy K. Kiyooka. Used by permission of Talonbooks.

Cover and text design by Jazmin Welch
Edited by Erín Moure
Poethics read by Patricia Salah
Copy edited by Shirarose Wilensky
Proofread by Alison Strobel

Printed and bound in Canada

Library and Archives Canada Cataloguing in Publication:
Title: Iron goddess of mercy : a poem / Larissa Lai.
Names: Lai, Larissa, author.
Identifiers: Canadiana (print) 20200322923 | Canadiana (ebook) 20200322931 |
    ISBN 9781551528441 (softcover) | ISBN 9781551528458 (HTML)
Classification: LCC PS8573.A3775 I76 2021 | DDC C811/.54—dc23

For Hong Kong
My sweet umbrella

She had some horses she loved.
She had some horses she hated.

These were the same horses.

JOY HARJO
"She Had Some Horses"

without fanfare
the procession of angels
have disappeared into
the ranks of the living

ROY KIYOOKA
"Five Poems of Resurrection"

You can't write about the furies.

COLM TÓIBÍN
Speaking on *Writers and Company*

1.

Dear Maenad, meet me halfway at the crossroads where we
played touch footsie our pedicures glistening bright in the
moonlight. Dear Monad when you were my one and homely,
we aired our uglies to ducklings wet as greenbacks aching for
a border crossing. Dear Mynah parroting the last politic, dear
miner, I'm digging deep for gold, for diamond dust, asbestos,
my best friend's girl. Dear Moonie, hugging the cult of the
belt the boot of the bat the bear and the bull full of it sully my
gully the grey bird rat of the sky screams dreaming of gullible
burgers as the market door swings open to the grey and rainy.
Dear Kool-Aid, Dear Gut Rot, Dear Deadhead singing where
have all the flowers gone? Dear Dust Bowl, Dear Chiang Kai-
shek, Dear Shrek your smile green, your antennae scan the
skies of our Distant Early Warning Line. Dear Monster Mash,
tear me to shredded chicken, I'm so hungry I could cry. Dear
Mourning has broken, dear token my best friend's one and
only, dear mayhem, dear Moonie howl at it while your vocal's
stoical, while the cord of your sword's still sharp and dark
as a clark's inkling recording rust and rebar, tea and totals,
Dear Moaner parroting the harp seal and munching flipper
pie, Dear Mailman staking your hot plot digging deeper
where the white man's dug before, I've been working on the
stale road haunting the crossroad where we burnt ghost
money smoking the stairway to heaving boulders rolled from

mountains dynamiting our break on through to the other's
mother the love of my lite flite blasting a rocket ship to venus.
Dear Dolly, gosh golly implicated in the hog's holly clearing
brush for democracy's prop prop propolis staging the metro's
underground for undocumented crossings while the bees
buzz around your head 'til you can't think straight and they're
measuring your cranium for uranium digging deeper than
down for the black gold to bomb your ass to kingdom kum
quat or some yung gai the vegetables of my digital LAN thirsty
as a burst oil pipe skyping me in.

Seek Peace find Labour

    Buzzing around windsock's

Empty hive

2.

Dear Occupation, know your station wastin' in Wong Nai
Chung Gap blastin' the mishap of opium's cornucopia the
dope of east asia co-prosperity no apology after the golly
of america's postwar reconstruction plus deduction paid by
the rough stamp of made in japan vs made in china bullying
fragrant harbour's ever open shop, no stop even on sunday my
hawker rushes her cart into hiding as cops bop your survival's
illegal watch the eagle and praise the rule of law always say
uncle when sam comes knocking no flocking or swarming in
hordes or perils stay feral and leave the critters to the army
of uniforms british, japanese or prc occupation's your vocation
your relation makes a paste of yellow flesh here to do picky
duty with fingers nimble 'til they stumble eyes precise until
they slant the cant of burnout under factory lights burning
special economic in sum jun, gow loong, chung king nest
of my marginal brothers watering the swamp paved over in
backwards rhetorics clean as the mean or mister blistering
all my black-haired sisters down to the last drop of blood,
pus, coffee or tea here's glee here's a plea my market's stark as
other blood marking nanking, manchukuo or hong kong on
christmas day our modern christian praying for deliverance
of the kind colonizer interned at stanley as all our brothers
stagger mass rape's estimation at ten thousand i don't want to
talk about it i was so unhappy then i'm happy now that i have

you little shoe and pretty dress my hair's a mess do you have to drive that ugly car star let's get away from him he's ignorant he doesn't know anything. and do you have lots of pretty friends in your nice school in new found land, new fin lund i wanted to go to school he made me stop at grade three i could have been smart like you like your mama all my children are so smart i never thought my life would turn out this good buy me another set of those pyjamas from zeller so comfy cheap a leap and pass me my chanel sweet smell of everything's gonna be alright.

It takes a Mountain

    To build a village at Yau Yat Chuen

An Embargo to lose it

3.

Dear Mask, maker of my other cover, I'm over the weather
wearing feathers as though my fine follicles could scale the
cell walls of tyrannosaurus rex. What hex? My dearest witches
code their spells to organize a future alphabet for one fine day,
make hay from moonshine to dress an army of gin drinkers at
Wong Nai Chung Gap. If we didn't eat apples, would we stop
feeling shame? I dove Private Benjamin to touch the clock of
the long now. My garden cajoles Eden Robinson to tell us how
it is. Mother knows that apples are not the only fruit though
she praises the five bumps at the bottom of delicious. In
season mangoes swing Luzon to Julie as grandfathers struggle
coolie to manager in economic zones offering no cover from
sun or gunboat diplomacy while Jimmy Lai makes his fortune
closing the gap between Chinese and Western fashion, parses
pasta's return for Giordano Bruno's cosmic pluralism the sun
that burns us only one sun among many. Whose workshop
worlds this revolution when the stakes are hot and high?
If Polo goes for horses and T-shirts how does angel hair
spaghetti touch wonton mein? What if cover and gender were
questions of reverb proud to disturb the foundation garments
of our feminine endings, show us the meat of our murder
growing over the bones that are stones? Would our arms be
prosthetic as armies extending the white man's labour to make
property out of sacred land? My hand runs free of its spider,

uncanny as a jar of jam. Dear Musk, wandering Elon of the electrical solution, can scent pay what sight cannot? When does my facial dressing make me real and when does my slant signal untrustworthy? I birth a river of stars slashing for scars to signal loyal. How am I s'posed to breathe through all this beauty? When the cover of COVID can't decide whether it's kinder to go outside or stay indoors? Who's keeping score, fifteen love in favour of Billie Jean King, the thing is, the kid is not my son.

Naked blade

        open wound

   read   Red   Redress

4.

Dear Moodiness working the intellectual railroad the frog and
pony show open for business open for booty playing footsie
with the cooties mark of the schoolyard god's her own father
and she don't even believe in 'im roll the rock over the opening
of my cave my củ chi tunnels the funnel of my widening drain,
Dear Marksman in the jungles of Borneo faking Chinese to
Japanese, dirty knees, dirty money of our Sinopec n PETRONAS
moan-digging the dirt of our home on Native land, Dear
TAZARA, Addis Ababa to Djibouti looting African earth
digging the dearth of the widening girth our hunger sprung
from an English thirst for tea. Dear Hestia my best friend's
hearth lit on the heath of your cliff the strange boy howling
opium to Cathay Pacific's honorific, the kow tow's go-down as
Japanese zeroes bomb the warehouses of Yeh Yeh's labour in
the fresh modern photo shop da tsap to steward through loyal
labour and the desire to do the ancestors proud. Dear Hustler,
shaking your kung fu spread wide and sweet as oriental
openings slanted for business in spite of what your emperor
daddy wanted, Dear Malwa sweet and deep as forever sleep
I've been working on the exploitative labour front my corded
back carrying catties for the rich man's bone, my fingers
nimble quick as candlesticks fiddling flowers etching iPhones,
Dear Labour, Dear Back Pain, sing me a song of the Middle
Temple the hemp the gentlemen of Verona, Dear Kona, Dear

Soma, the body ticks its lickin' pickin' its quick while the jackpot's a sweet 99 million. I wear my therapist's avatar, my politic's meat puppet a drop for the crabs in the pulpit while the octopus waves its metro card at the South China Morning Post conceding to PRC propaganda.

Blast Rocky Mountains for cash

Railway tunnel unites Whites only

Leaves cousins in ditch

5.

Hey five-year-old village girl disposable as razors after
American stubble bursts your bubble, my hubble sees far as
mars as jupiter hooping the old men of endless war to even
the Cold War score, Hey Hot Dog, Hey Pol Pot, Hey Chairman
Mao after the how of your Long March your love for the
people swinging empty as bottles after the glass is broken
after the beatings after the Confessions the disappearances
the slashed tongues and cracked skulls, Dear Complicity your
felicity's a kitty's mirror cute as a cut smile on pink plastic
and beautiful dreamer wake unto me, I scare my therapist's
gesture civil as personal boundaries flashing a forged passport
at the hoarder's border. Sing me a song of the Knights Templar
the flight's exemplar, manufacturing samples for the moving
market. Dear Rosy, Dear Tarot, root of my personal potato, I
cross my time's centred present, Dear Judgment, Dear Hanged
Man drawing us from the hard walls of our ancient caves,
horses gallop for scallops race track or silk road, belts bet on
ducky's luck, jockey for transition even as our radios phone
home. Dear deer, your innocent forest sprouts ghost moss and
old growth, as linear time breaks its boiler. Door deer at the
threshold seeks mesh to reweb your mycorrhizae, mushroom
of my creamy soup the loop hoops us scooping the blooper's
real reel.

Citizen Science

Neoliberal Capital

A woman limping

6.

Dear May Day, I'm falling, help I need more bodies more
selves to sell out to the Man he's multiple and wants my blood
my heart my kidney my liver my cunt my shunt my front to
back and up the bum, Dear Moo Day, the cows can't take it
anymore milked and meted out to the highest bidder in steaks
and bakes rump roasts and tenderloin, my sweetest dearest
as innocent brown-eyed girls, Dear Foreplay, I forgot my
prophylactic I'm haptic wired on Starbucks touch me quick
my Queequeg's thirsty for the thump of the captain's peg leg,
my Achilles heel was my Achilles heel and the battle's just
begun, ten years at war or twenty Dear Mui Lan waving your
jolly green Dear Disney, Dear Friendly Giant, I'm compliant
hemmed in by the haul of your totalizing system, Dear Stem
Cell, Dear Cowbell dialing the old rotor to get that long-
distance feeling. Dear Brow, Dear Beating I'm sleeting up to
here with the thick of it, the quick of it, the closed border of
my marginal being the wasp buzz in the wall of the house,
the skitter of the mouse and the fast trap we set with peanut
butter to slap the flap splat that little brown furry furious
as unwanted only here because of you and your waste and
your warmth the house of your greedy cover. Dear Rat that
ate the trapped mouse, Dear Brother Rat that ate the peanut
butter in the other trap, it clapped your body too big to die
you skittered for hours blood brain spatter over walls wires

hammers boots camping gear hooks and tarps and Edward had to clean because I wouldn't even look.

East Vancouver House

    Exceeds borders of Foundation

Happy rodents feast

7.

Dear House that Giuseppe built we ate your plums n figs
n blighted pears years after you loved and left them. Dear
Turquoise Stucco beside Pink Stucco, Dear Miami in East
Van, Dear Brazen Drug Dealer with your array spread over
the hood of your good old Chevy in the back alley over which
we saw the bungalow fall to the dozer with curtains still in
the windows and the grey sixplex burst instantly from earth.
Dear Kale and Purple Beans, Dear Salvaged Cupboards, we
had so many to choose from. You were all such a pain in the
neck but I loved you anyway. Dear Overwork, Dear Racial
Representation, your committees have my pity and I bite my
thumb. Dear Class Size, Dear Accreditation, your frame drains
me, Dear Student Bodies the liver of the system digging your
twenty-year-old choice for voice or paycheque, heckling from
the back or absorbing from the front, do you remember the
day I killed myself laughing over your discovery of allegory?

Rainforest City

      Hallucinates Heap of Gold

Old ginkgo grows nuts

8.

Dear Matmos, Dear Economy, Dear Collective Hallucination,
abomination, retaliation, do you remember when? The time
before your slippery fist gripped us made us debt puppets
flubbing justice through the sense of the dollar, the spike
of the collar, the fleas of the market on a lark through our
bloodstreams desperately seeking a port to plug us in. Dear
Butt Plug, Dear Shithead, we beat you to the DIY crafting
in factories the mud of capital otherwise known as plastic
the fantastic of your twentieth-century dream, all the junk
that held you in its loving arms promising forever for at
least five minutes before swimming to the widening gyre,
the Pan Pacific hotel sighing sails and orcas as we flush our
mush unprocessed down the open drain. Gain's the same
all brain curling its convolutions n gripping them tighter
than whiteness seeking its new level as the cherry coke of
colonialism bungles its last drop, its sock hop revealed to
reproduce hegemonies abundant as kittens itchin' for a burlap
sack, a stone, a mewl and moan, cuter than a cut and hard to
drown. Dear Clown, wolf howling for candy striped stockings
dense as calves, while punters split sides of beef, a coral reef,
the chief grief of our sea change. A fathom for the father, why
bother, there's moths in the cauldron bubbling toil for oil as
the sands make mordor out of boreal even as land defenders
paddle for justice. Just us, but our we's a scattered and surly

lot half pegged to the dollar's holler, some writhe wriggling
to get free while the other half close eyes and bow down to the
id of the giant squid twit inking to a mastery of muffins and
stuffin' his deep pockets with the flesh of the down and brown
the earth's dearth hitching fear to the dollar like there's no
tomorrow.

Tao holds Time's Circle

Turtle Oracle pattern

Ghost river shifts rocks

9.

Dear Tomorrow, your zombies are already upon us munching
the mesh of our towers and boardrooms our hobbits and
hovels heave a hunger you can't resolve. Dear Hungry Ghost at
the Crossroads, looking for lonely travellers with haversacks,
however empty we can empty you further. Your burthen's a
bother a brother a collar tryna make a dollar outta fifteen—
your mother's a moth waving her butterfly net knowing
already the tao of change snatching the coy joy of crab with
cracked pepper or a walk among the golden chain trees
aware of the monster at the edge of the garden yet closing a
deliberate eye. She pardons, holding the circle, having long
stopped counting heads cut and heads sprouted, not doubting
the eternal return.

Chinaman's luck

Aces pulled from Stacked Card Deck

Mah-jong flowers   Pung!

10.

Dear Motor engine of my one and only, dear soma in a coma
I'm stoned on white collar labour a favour da tsap to steward
to businessman scholarship kid to squid on a stick grilled with
salt and spicy bean paste. Dear Moana, surfing black hair flat
vs curly, swinking the difference capital slices wash the rice
parboiled jasmine basmati or thai you tell a story like kokuho
rose or suspicious texana vicious as gen mod's modified your
bod to fit cap's script the prop of property hopping up the type
of torture meted and passed on down the daunting hauntings
that bite our hearts and keep us apart. Dear UpStart Dear
StartUp parting people where the hair divides, we're saturated
in narrative the bitten apple of capital the hype of whiteness
blights us modified generations before we hit the table
committed to the fable of Abel because cane's already cut and
shipped and before that the bodies the same ship unequal
arrangements, key horror of stacked in cords or boarded as
hordes the murder of mordor the blight of the condor fond as
the arsenal of pounds and dollars bonds and sellers whetting
the machete on the killing floor. The girl next door primps
for pimp, swells for seashells, rustles for reverb, lip-syncs the
story of tokyo rose, elevates stain to colour full fabric. Too
slow to see the signal, I floor the pedal of capital dial my smile
to suit the while as gas gushes fast to the pass of no return. I
gasp my clasp on the past lost in the race for place, crash my

glass ceiling or last illusion the contusions of the brain drain
calling same when we all know the difference.

Way down Portugal

    Cove Road fishing wharf sniffs

Old Fragrant Harbour

11.

Dear Moon, my bloodline rushed to earth in time with your
table, I grow my leaves and vines on your quiet rotation and
orbit, leave the exorbitant Gregorian to sunny invaders avoid
their parades through streets and forests of gorgon time my
sign snakes to rivers underwater ghost worlds swimming fish
our scaly ancestors waiting for the dollar to run its course.
Our course is deeper and sweeter trenching beneath oceans to
flow to bide our time tectonic though grenades and genocides
break us over and over we break and reconnect and break
and reconnect segmented and whole and the hole dug deep
enough to swallow time. Dear Mane, shaggy as the heads of
lions guarding the gates of our homes on native land our loans
on dative sand awaiting the remand old China hands getting
back on the boat we're no longer fresh off comefromaways
indentured or investors astronauting in on the back of the
holler, Dear Molar chomping down on the bit or biting a piece
of the pie in the sky the dream made real through relations of
exchange, Dear Midas, Dear Muffler shutting down the wrong
voices, my ghost river's a reverse of the waking nightmare
forced by the son of the sun of a gun of rum and sugar, tea
and tobacco the grades the priesthood teaches us to want
judgment from above to secure our places buffering the
suffering even if we hate them. We trade pinches for knowing
where we stand. What if you don't stand where you think you

stand? If you've lived your life walking on property but never setting foot on land? What if the land has been tasked with masking despots as princes? Rise and rinse them, choose the substance of revelation—tea or water? Milk or murder? Crows take us further than telephone lines teach birds to swim and fish to fly doctor the squalor of order to reveal an older order beneath, bequeath the go of the flow to the moon ones, the womb ones and tomb ones we women shimmer in the dim gestating a softer light that permeates concrete illuminating the tooth of illusion.

Wolf blood moon howls Mad

As domestic Dog

Begs raw meat from Mom

12.

Dear Murder, herding us like cattle into the lineups of death,
Dear Ship, Dear Quip, brutality of ledger and software, the
orchestration of it conducting death music for deadheads,
generating desire and dearth, converting the dearth to a
machine of suffering, buffering only those you mark as human
in other words other murderers glorifying blonds and bonds
in markets and mansions consumption the gumption in the
pluck of settlement whose betterment pegged first to the
body then collared to the dollar the divide and conk in guns
chains bombs and rhetoric co-opting in the aftermath. Dear
Manager, parsing out your us or them, bordering against the
laws of thermodynamics, animate markers to make bodies of
experience scrub ghosts, make them new again stew again our
flavour of the moth rages in street and boardroom passed out
in the classroom on the killing floor of our own making we're
baking the heat of it too neat for the mess you made when you
went away when you came back in the guise of benevolence
your heart on your silk or cotton sleeve bereaved in the
aftermath that was always the ongoing as we take a licking
and keep on picking up after you unless you cut us burn us
waterboard chain or torture glass kneel us rape us smile now
I don't understand why you're so upset.

The Rules were broken

Your brown eyes are Small

It must have been you

13.

Dear White Lady with rights to footsteps, dear board, dear
neighbour, it's really too late to have guests over, dear teacher,
dear parking meter, lock me in my box and make me quiet,
make me compliant to the game of another one down and
another one down, dear co-opted co-op, dear chicken coop,
take the space but don't move in it, don't you know the rules
are for you and only you, looping me to the purity of my
ideals. Dear Done and Dusted, Dear Rust, dear Pus, a pox
on you for learning me your harangue, as rush and gush
of mother tongue lost in translation gods 'er own father
and you're back in grade two stay out of the circle or come
over but you're not allowed in the house, dear carpet, dear
underlay, durian and the curse of purses, dear witches, dear
cancer, i know your girlfriend is living there, dear scrutiny,
dear mutiny, we have our reasons but it's never the one
we'll give. Dear Workshop sometimes there are casualties in
co-ops on campuses on buses in courtrooms and this time
it's you. Sorry so sorry oh golly suzy here's a fortune cookie
for your trouble. Dear Departmental Compartment, Dear
Representation, Dear Committee, Dear Museum that already
knows all about it, Dear Buddhist begging Shirley to accept
that the white man won, Dear what kind of psychology does
your trauma belong to, Dear don't Speak until the guests are
gone, Dear Curb your anger and we'll throw you crumbs, the

guff of it, enough of it, Dear Holy Brother parsing proximity to
the father, my place on the ladder, most definitely beneath his,
Dear fucker, my precious pornographer, lining Asian girls up
before the philosophers to test the quality of their underwear,
dear Judgment hoarding the plunder and asking me to prove
my worth, dear Duckworth, dear Hogwort, the harm of the
charm smokes the girth of the curse I left so you'll never sleep.

In high damp Summer

Donald's puts out glowing bins

Peaches fragile sweet

14.

Dear Migrant, Rita had all the language to help you but I
couldn't because I flushed my mother down the assimilation
drain, I'm sorry I saw you as the ghost of Christmas past and
present and I was you and you were me but we weren't all
together I gave my identification card to the colonizer the
opium pipe I skyped my village in three generations ago when
the twentieth century descended and the Qing opened China
for a bidding war, when tea debt became opium debt and
imperial armies burned Hakka rebellions, workers and village
folk dreaming of modernity only to pay the patriarchy as we
still do daily and we ran for survival or we ran for opportunity
and the two weren't necessarily that far apart. Dear Rusty
Ship, Dear Salt Water, Dear Burnaby Correctional Centre, the
least I could do was drive and cook and march, so I did that,
'til my girlfriend thought I was having an affair, 'til some dude
wanted an affair and she thought you were him the stupid
drama of it I know guilt's a useless emotion but it snowed me
under. Where are you now and your son who hated you for
taking him away from his father in China and who found the
streets while you worked three jobs to keep a roof and prove
to the state I belong to that you were worthy. Rita says: *I can't
bear it and I can't not bear it.* We sublimate under the weight
of the plunder. I blunder my subaltern power, make the future
under conditions of my own bruising.

Democratic in-

    stit stitches garment up

Same old body

15.

Dear Bother, we dream the same dream except that in it you're
the king of the hill and I know my place, dear burden asking
me to hold you up when you can't do the same, do you know
how heavy you are? When you lay it on, when you can't get
enough, when you use the pain of others as cover for your ego
hunger? As deflection of critique? When you know the white
man is watching, when you know they want us sad then dead
want our taxidermied skins for their work of representation
reproduction? And you want credit for discovery? As in, you
met me, and thought you were so clever. When you channel
our collective labour for your own glory, query credentials
and bona fides to hide your lack, I'm sorry, enough's enough,
the nerve of it, the waste of it, the quick and dirty haste of
it. Everybody wants absolution, everybody wants justice.
Everybody wants to be clean and Seen. You've been what
you've been, fed stars to machine, it's about labour then and
labour now, the Cold how of it, the hours in towers that make
your power hour your glow in the dark subatomic neurotic
hungering to the bottom of every sister's barrel how many can
you eat before the store is empty cores and spirits crushed
faster than the master plan can orchestrate.

Oh yeah and also

    I will not get Over it

Easily   so there

16.

Dear Brother, I saw you at murder's border and cogged a
complicated relation. We're sport for the Man and his can
of Spam making meat of the id id ideology in his head. Dear
Birder, I saw you girded for flight held down by the bite the
chomp the fight the blight the mean and measly spite of it. I
stood best as I could it wasn't enough never enough from the
bluff behind which I'm parked I punch it I cinch it I pinch
wish with Bruce I had a rocket launcher stauncher than the
hour of power the Man's bestowed to exercise only as he
wishes the score of the war of the rep rep repetition of rrr rrrr
representation spin around wooden doll the sandman's optics
caught us in the sin twirl whirling as we dig for the thread of
genealogy positive or negative polarizing the battery the wish
that I was there for you back in the gist of the mist sifted for
the howl of now. If time's not the line of the border or the
hashtag of history blistering its attack if it's as the elders say
a circle that time past permeates always already time present
could I lay my body on the railroad tracks stop my brothers
dynamiting holes in the mountains? All the tracks we built,
then and now, in Africa, Asia, Turtle Island, could we take
them back find another way to survive the dearth the braid the
China trade? Stop the ship and deploy a different ship? Or stay
the fuck home as the emperor wanted, self-sufficient if sexist?
Drive the mushroom cloud back down into earth, mycorrhizal

net webbing footsteps of organisms push back carbon
footprint of desire machine burning from within and without
driving us to the armageddon only puritans want? Gaunt
as ghosts we haunt the crosses of history preceding Christ
preceding even the Hudson's Bay store, East India Company
and Jardine Matheson. What love could smooth the scar the
Man keeps opening for business self-replicating system as
downward spiral? We went viral but warfare's germs exceeded
our best intentions.

With Hiromi Sea-to-Sky

   tread rot sniff for golden Sign

tankard mushroom butts to surface

17.

Dear Meat Monster, I want my money back, no denying the
eternal return of desire for passport house boots and fruits. I
longed for arrival. I wanted my innocence and eat it too with
XO sauce, in broth or fried in hot oil, crunchy tender as baby
octopus, beef tendon, the slippery lick of jellyfish on a platter
of cold meats. I'm beat. The christian lean we gleaned to crack
the pepper of the emperor's absolute power has backfired,
I'm a hoser a poser stuck in the loop of the wannabe buzzing
around an empty hive. What five to get high with, sigh with,
hung out to dry with? I'm afraid of what I Feel, the affect of
the man zips through me fast and neurotic as my myopic's
ontic, I'm gutted by the flutter of ugly feelings. I reel, I
congeal, so sorry, but sorry's castle has already been co-opted
by the state and capitalized as stable economy. My astronomy
swings from the star machine I wish would rust and turn to
dust or butter toast. A roast for the ghosts crowding doorways
without papers bleeding from the body and beyond. I return
my clean uniform eternally for the gristly bits, the love, the
responsibility, my lineage knows the chop suey of invention,
the few dishes for many extended by rice in rich times
and water in lean. I welcome the dirt as long as the water's
kept clean. What am I suturing? I dream my grandmother
sewing the garment to fit the body, unhooking, restitching
through growth spurts and wounds. I'm wound bound to the

bodhisattva of go and flow the double affect of the go-between
haptic as happenstance reckoning with history as reports
from deep time roll tectonic and earth waves shower me with
truth's debris.

This bicycle's Not

A wheel Barrow legislating

Backyard chickens

18.

Dear Machine, can one machine be medicine for another machine? When the biopolitic sticks when the necropolitic kicks, I ache for liberal love know already that god above and capitalism from below have blown the coop, have stoned the co-op, enthroned the blowhard laying out the roulette of the blowfish. Dear Globefish, swimming your way to the scales of just us, bust us, your lust for time is palpable, cycling the girth of our worth the jelly belly of the planet itself. Round and round and round she goes where she stops is where the bee sucks slamming the ham of our happy pen. No time like the wasn't. No crime without cousins. Bee's buzzin' fuzzy as wuz a bear. I stare for carin', blarin' my flugelhorn for narcissus, oh delicate mirrorflower shining in water. I fall to the call of the child the care of the mild siloed in bile, stuck at the turnstile all the while crying for what I lost. The cost of nostalgia: myalgia, the ruined body returned in the aftermath of too much thinking.

Sledgehammer refracts

    frog   River   scorpion

Last glance before smash

19.

Dear Magic, fragile and tragic as jook-sing's bling bling
ringing the bells of hell. Dear Ebb and Swell, riding the tide
of tomorrow, bombed by the Japanese for belonging to the
British, embargoed by America for belonging to the Commies,
returned to the poverty of your youth when the go-down
went up in flames, you built reputation instead of capital only
to lose the hoi of Poy's polloi when the curtain of imbroglio
fell in Korea's DMZ. Number Six you count your siblings, one
left: Lucky Eight. Father lays out a single memory: day trip
to Uncle Eight's to eat lettuce wrap. One Two Three Four
Five and Seven gone to leavened bread, if it's painful we don't
talk about it, why pass the grief on to the children, starved
thin as embargo's cargo, watch Key Largo and dream instead
the beauty of Bacall. Whisper the better stories: great-
grandmother's Kuomintang husband who fought the Japanese
then fought the civil war up North and was dismissed when
the Communists won. Run south with your soldier brothers.
In a hole in the earth, or tunnel or trench you forged a pass to
port yourselves back over the British line, safe in the arms of
the colonizer or at least back to the bus depot of family happy
as the other sister Buddhist lay, wealthy with her little room in
the old lady house on the mountainside, no spouse no grouse,
waiting for the light of the other enlightenment. Dear Murder,
not to be passed on, instead we remember the joy of the Three

Musketeers: Poy, Lai and the Englishman the lotto's photo
making joy in the aftermath of opium, the grade of trade not
yet liberal member back before Hirohito before the bombs
the scrapes in Happy Valley where the racehorses still run,
and we roll the dice and roll the dice and wasn't Auntie
Two on Mother's side lucky to marry into the family of the
architect of the Casino Lisboa in Macau where during the
war Mother's father ran with his tennis racquets to escape
the Japanese who thought he hid pro-British propaganda
in the handles. The Japanese soldiers came for Poh Poh,
chased her around a table, Auntie Three remembers, laughing
to hide. Does that mean she was raped? I don't want to talk
about it, I was so unhappy then, I'm happy now, why would
I want to remember? On the hydrofoil to Lantau: See those
English people? Follow them. They know where the good
seats are. Sugar Plum Fairy, it's scary, tinkling my way to
Englishness. I want to take you to the temple while I still can.
But you climb the 268 steps to the Buddha on your own. My
legs, it's too late. Oh Poh Poh, don't you know the Temple of
Heaven Buddha's not for me? It's Kuan Yin all the way.

Surfing late night twenty years on

Find maternal village on Hotwire Cheap Hotel

4.3/5 rating 10 yuan popular ticket Nanhai Kuan Yin

20.

Dear Southern Ocean, salt potion of my motion's insufficient
vote, I taste by rote, a surfeit of Inglish that compensates
yet dims my mother tongue, the fumble of latin rumbling
suffixes as though the shun of my shush could free me from
all you were fleeing. I forgot before the memory had content,
let rot the fishy horror and mix with chilies to make a paste
for coating fresher meat. The sheet she tossed to blank the
Confucian tangle, new feminist with a third world inkling,
blinking newborn to a better future. What suture, dear Angel
of History, my feckless wreckage floats on a shifting current,
mistress of the backstroke swimming for a world record,
unable to see for the foam kicked up by her own feet. My
Hakka boat sets sail for another coast, boasting mushrooms,
scallops and bean curd sheets as though the beasts of your
waters could beat the Manchu occupation. What peace could
you lease? Will the Jesus you've borrowed for your vision
release you if the white man won't let go? When modernity
hangs its rice paddy hat on the hook of one god, is that the
bait your fish will take? I'm still waiting to walk on land.
The i ching too traps fishes before releasing them back to the
watery flow of time. What if, in spite of everything forgotten,
the whole fabric remains swimming or stitching in fish form?
Could I open my mouth, release another poetry, a lifetime's
worth of pent-up Cantonese?

Inside the Black egg

    White and yellow   inside the Brown

Egg black and green

21.

Dear Tragic, putting two and two together, the brother who died. Before I was born. He used to beat her and beat all the other kids except for me, he loved me, I don't know why. I watch him, eat the jue yook bang she's cooked with preserved duck egg, salty and tender over a bowl of hot rice. She's a terrible cook, he says as he chows on down, old man antennae waving. I recall the cockroach in the bedroom he killed with his shoe when I was five, my first mute visit to Breezy Terrace and my last. The cockroach was four inches long. We were all so impressed by the shoe's slap and squelch. I hate him, I hate him, let's leave him at home. So happy now that I have you, look I got you a ticket for The Nutcracker. Oh Poh Poh, Tchaikovsky's so colonial, I want to go to the wet market, the night market, the Kuan Yin temple. I need her cover for the slap of come over but you're not allowed in the house. Why do you want to see these dirty things? I'll take you to Park Lane, the newest mall, so beautiful, I'll buy you a dress, a purse, a car—I don't need all that fancy stuff, Sugar Plum Fairy dances, enhanced by too much love as suffering buffers the real deal of the history they've wriggled out of gathered round the lazy Susan. Get it honey, the drive for money, it's pride over pain the remainder of the memory the sadness of what can't be said. Don't speak of the dead. Silence the violence passed on down, to make the shame a gain. On the backs of others? Oh brother, these are the jollies of melancholy's deck the halls.

Trade lunar for Solar

New year for christmas to Get

Modern as someone else's History

22.

Dear Money, substance of love and sadness, please flow
sweet as the same China twice. No dice, though you roll
and roll and roll back the rim the past erupts as doubles and
bubbles, taking the pulse of the husk at dusk or two minutes
to midnight, snacking on dishes the previous generation left
out of care, not grasping the principles of rot. Dear Moonie,
too hot for the Sunday funnies and too cool for rule Britannia,
structural oppression is one thing, pure despotism's another,
as brothers gather in fluthers, pulse through waters of our
parents' transport red beautiful as sunset after the forest fire
and wired on Starbucks trying to capture the world whale
before it changes again the same ocean twice. Sting you or
bling you depends on the bandwidth of Facebook the shadow
of your digital signature as pushing hands reach out to touch
someone. He practised his kung fu on the tennis court, curt
as fifteen love to deuce, sluicing juice from dregs of empire
trying to predict the next best thing.

The problem is fascia

Thin Sticky membrane that slings

The body's meat

23.

Dear Freedom of Speech, you leech grinching under cover as
democratic process, I saw you on the counter at Montana's
wiping beef grease from your beard. Weird or feared, your
fury's dreary, trolling beneath the bridge of birds webbing our
digital sky. You swing the pubic of public opinion spinning the
rotten onion one fart at a time, lining your pockets with the
proceeds of Wall Street greed, feeding at the trough of rough
golf and grim bills passed by bullies in the gamers chambers
disingenuous corridors of power. You were beautiful once,
a bunch of daisies a bed of poses, loaning your armour to
all and sundry, as part of the parcel, colonialism stressed as
democracy. I'm not too shy to wear that dress battered and
tattered, ill-fitting in the hip and crotch, and screaming gotcha
mad as a crow on the hatter's wire every time the wrong body
steps outta line. It's fine, I bide my time, dreaming signs and
pigeons passing on the truth of the park stark as cop cars
patrolling my neighbour's hood. Gratitude says be good, we
thought you'd be nice, expedient, obedient take the blunt
force of maxwell's pilfered hammer sold down the shiver or
horse traded down by the tracks where hacker's anonymous
and raised up only posthumously so some yung gai can make
a career drink beer paid by your fear. Clarity, charity, the
mock of democracy is that you're only meant to adore it,
adore the white man's exploration. The habit of inhabitation

is the straitjacket of race and know your place. Face it, the
encounter's only for the chinaman if she wipes it down herself.

How to sweet-talk a persimmon

  Wait 'til it's soft peel Bitter skin

Slurp down flesh

24.

Dear Mrs Malaprop, granting officer after my own heart, your
lark lays forms to administrate every second of my becoming.
I strum my pipa to accommodate your background music,
score the movie before rights have tightened to render my
legality dubious as points of both departure and arrival. I
strive for perpetual carnival holding rockets at the cape, long
as I can hide my eyes 'til the big surprise. I could never do the
cryptic crossword, but I leave clues on the sole of every shoe,
grab my geiger to test the radiation pattern of your essential
self. Did you intend for me to arrive at the state fully fledged?
Or should my Papagena arc a little closer to the sun? I like the
error in your feathers. This experimental body tries Bhabha's
door for the absurdity of war in third space, third national
rational as substituting sweet potato for rice when times are
lean. Hope the water's clean. Rita shudders at the crack for
fracking, despairs tailings ponds and hydroelectric rupturing
the flow of the same river twice. The cover of difference
masquerading as same tracks time's trouble back to the point
of no return, original dirt where the secret slipper first made
its mark.

River yellow

Mud skin   mud muscle

Mud   rock   bone

25.

Dear Dumpster of Assumption, your gumption stumps me.
I'm bumptious seeking the gumbo of my Biloxi neighbour, we
stray, seeking the how of our connection Acadia to Mississippi
the blue dreams of her unearthed ceremonial mounds.
Fire's burning churning my desire to remember Angelique,
seeking the how of memory cut by the rifle's butt or the
multicultural container shipping me outta there before I can
see the connection, deny the distorted reflection, sectioned in
separate laws and separate forms of incarceration, declaration,
nomination, stationing our crossroads on different levels
the jenga of my meringue to your merengue, your exclusion
to my exclusion documented in books cooked for different
market segments or sequences in sequined gown and town
or down and brown shoving our noses in it. Draw nearer in
the gloaming singing the loon of the tune harmonious or dis
our cycles out of sync with merry I remember berries without
Beothuk whose knowledge found its way into my yellow
hands and there to join the tar sounds of our mutual assured
destruction, the suction of greed's vampiric vacuum drinks the
links of our bonaparte we build our bona fides as walls to shut
out the hunger of liberalism's washout and pass cards that
can't be stamped the connection is only there in what you feel,
but how do you know your feelings are the real deal spun by
the propaganda of the goose's gander, the last emergency stop

before europe's parsing engine, the jumbo jet burst the sound
barrier that pops our eardrums so we only hear the fire's roar,
the score of the bore tangling us in the gulag of accounting,
shoving forms to shut us up, insisting on an attitude of
gratitude even as our sisters are incarcerated in camps of the
man's making. Stake the pyre sired by the grief and frustration
of the wrong ministrations. How armageddon returns again
and again to reiterate the gains of the same machine twice as
mounts and staines reproduce the power bower closing eyes
to the cries that resonate ten times as loud. The cloud that
shrouds the advance guard of my social's high tea praying
for stray dogs and perogies, a hoagie with gravy staves off
the navy as the boys of abstraction gatekeep the route to the
voices of before. Say at least the names of the people who
host us, Musqueam, Tsleil-Waututh, Squamish, Tsuut'ina,
Kainai, Piikani, Blackfoot as soot from the Columbia River
Gorge, Squilax, Xat'sull, Williams Lake falls on our heads,
are the flakes so snowy or fragile? I'm agile, waving my flag for
the sjws holding the fort against the alt-right bringing blight
through the door of the liberalisms we thought we wanted,
haunted by the posts of Christmas past.

Does fire remember

                Twice-trashed tabula

Life of Past garbage

26.

Dear Martyr, I lay my bod on the tracks that Jack built hacked by the sojourner uncles through territories Musqueam Stó:lō Stl'atl'imx Nlaka'pamux Secwépemc. I'm good 'til I'm not 'til the fear gets the better of me I claim the brain drain selfsame with a game of chess queen to bishop six and the door swings open to a phantasmagoric wonderland of waste the mushroom makes me tall and small too much and not enough as every orifice tells the truth squirting text and fluids the mammary wash of memory hemming and hawing at the border of sense. No fence on the same river twice as time circles my ankles the world snake liquid linking me to the blink of Sky Woman, Lee says we scattered across these Pacific territories kinning kind and unkind as the roll of the go and flow. What we share: everybody eats. But east of "Put it back the way you found it" we've mucked it, stuck in the loop of hot Chinese money another liquid link only real in the nimble fingers of Chinese girls fiddling fake flowers circuits needles numbers text sewing machines and dicks like there's no quick pick but the tao of the Dow cycling always back to the Nu Wa of my dreams. Maenad Martyr screams it, Dear Phoenix how many times can I reconstitute these damn ashes? Sad and had my moon bay stays waiting for the wolf at the door, taking score of the more and more I scream my dream and screen my preen hungry like the goof too tired to get fancy with the dance of the nonces. I rage in my cage the angriest woman awake in the iron box passing the pox the plague the tuberculosis to my grandfather for his insult to my grandmother after the death of her mother and sisters you dead TB ghost the intimate meanness of it as he takes scissors to the carefully fitted cheongsam she scrimped for and the hours of stitching to stave off grief the helpless greenness Dear Shrek what heck your love pegs me to the horror of her occupied body. Was his hat the imperial rapist's or did it come from my Hakka great-grandmother who paid the village boys to let him beat them up? Her determination to build a strong son protect the happy heart and hearth the roiling sum of oil son of toil harassed and harried by the rotating door of invaders? Dear Maenad Martyr, born on a bed of word nails, I love you for your ferocious hope and loyalty, full of fear you charge the door sword in one hand and a plate of chow mein in the other oh Virtuous Virgin, Iron Maiden, Goddess of Gold and Bitter Tea.

I stitch this cheongsam

At the border of sense mending Rifts

In space-time continuum

27.

Dear Cheongsam, Whose flesh do you stitch when you insert
your needle? She taught me how to wind fibre around steel,
stitch the knot into silk or cotton, the bottom-feeder of my
education the language of thread. What dread? In another
county women coded a whole language in new shoes, feet to
earth as the twentieth century pitched a few rough diasporans
kiting seeds into other dresses, we live both sides of the
stitch, doubled over laughing 'til we cry. Dear Girl Next Door,
what stride would pride us? To opt self-comber before the
cat of the hermeneut's gorilla? In a language made of thread
mind matters shattering glass ceilings to shower us in real
shards. My pard's got spots. I dot the rot with code to grow
new critters from litter. I spit, I dither, flowers in a fluster as
I muster movement to groove the pavement. Rita likes grass
that pushes up through cracks but both concrete and buried
roots are real. Don't wanna seal the deal and solidify the
inside out. I pry, I spy, drink Canada Dry to slip the noose of
untrustworthy and brink citizenship's uneven habit, Maenad's
rabbit out the hoot of her magical top. Old Long Ears sprints
the distance of our Long March while she inks a little blue
in the starch to make our collars and sneakers whiter than
white. Blue bunny chooses red pill swig a bit of moonshine for
Chang O, exiled for the arrogance of doing the archer under.
I blunder as Maenad shoots boosters for space on three two

one zero, hero of the feral paring her latest garment down to
garden's finest feather.

magpie chatter

awkward squawk

what grace your tail's blue shimmer

28.

Dear Saint Iris facing the virus of where I couldn't look my
reflection's bloody glare death bright and mutilated in the light
of red sun violence, I'm silent though it protects me not a whit
don't quit you haunt my monster clamouring in her cage of
rage my holy Asian kettled by the head of the baby hooked on
the imperial bayonet blood streaming from eye sockets floats
Cheshire grin thin and mad as grief on a stick fog memory
dense as flesh. Dear Apocalypse how a thousand yellow bodies
blasted up in the dirt as a sign of drugged-out American
madness I quiver water ghost of the same River Kwai riding
the back of the world snake earthquake rumble of our fracked
and finite future. Dear Fishmonger, the war was cold only for
the white man alt-right in tight pants never acknowledging the
cost of greed guaranteeing our safety pin only after gorging on
our hunger. Dear Gorgon how love slips away on duty's back
scales not for just us prove first your super hum n intention
only for attendants of the full subjective table able-bodied and
labelled already the red tape of exception stands you up for a
fight. Dear Protestant, send me to a contest I was never with
or against my taint plays polo on a different plane we chain
daisies awake at the iron dock waiting for the shipping lane
to shunt my interchangeable container sing in Inglish to the
changeling foxing her wily way outta here only to get boxed
anew. Am I safe in my iron box? Air's thin as plot thickens

stickin' the knife in and I twist wriggle against the regulations designed to keep me from the corridors where the real decisions are made as to who's played for the chance to dance the next ring float like madame butterfly dreaming she's a man a ham a can of spam or some other brother howling grief and rage to the false sage who's already turned their back.

Duck the Dialectic

Before trolls call you Chicken

So much batter under the bridge

29.

Dear Hannah, no sage at all but "totalitarianism has discovered a means of dominating and terrorizing human beings from within" thin as occupation congee and held together by propaganda slander of super eggo waffling on about holes in the griddle as middle kingdom swings to oozing eye of wanna be that guy that shuts the people down to thousands of millennia arching the crap of patrie particles article over the suf of self and sluicing the juice of a hundred million Chinese girls Confucian disposable and too filial to fight back. Fuck that, I'm gathering an army of the harmed, alarm bells ringing at last awake to the iron cock. I mean the old rooster in need of a booster shot or rocket or finally his place on the docket for all the times he's sold us cheap to the West foxing the con of silk or tea or china plates to stuff already stuffed pockets fuller than bullish as the wolves of gull street rat us out again. As you say the terror comes from within our fascist longings to hang our O out Maenad Martyr to Maenad Martyr racing our buckets to the well's bottom. Crabs claw our back dream wrack and tidal rot as preferable to plastic pail, back crawling angel of history towed under dreams of shore as rivers flow to ocean currents wet with ghosts travelling translucent as live fish dreaming one mind one muscle flip down deeper than Gulf Stream cling by teeth to cool our primate disaster.

As night kingdoms

Chu and Shu purify in Opposition

Sisters stitch cut flesh

30.

Dear Polar Bear panning critics as cap melts your pelt levels to
rising sea once svelte now mangy endangered as autopoietic
shock cogs of our ecological clock break down, link emissions
to atmosphere to ocean currents depositing heat in all the
wrong places disrupting the pattern of your liquid or solid,
I'm stolid wielding my shield as though blue cross could go on
forever to the never of Wonderland in which the tower I build
stands forever while the world collapses around it, confound it
kick your one cod to the seal's last meal iron goddess of mercy
in the connective tissue not issue of your polar mouth saying
south when you mean the girth of the north the first thirst of
everybody eats. How do your dialectics shred relation? Station
to station, one maenad at a time? Lining your reputation with
victory bonds of another when everybody knows the good
guys lost cost of being boss I lose you lose nursing our bruises
while the doctors of destruction go on raising the stakes and
remakes guarding avant devant as polar goes solar and bears
fly up to touch the sun.

Social justice under High capitalism:

I put you in your Place

Before you can put me in mine

31.

Dear Achilles, you heel, leave me reeling at the edge of the
battlefield, your colours show in showers plow me under just
in time to get stomped by the boot what a hoot I thought you
loved me but it was only for hovering above or taking cover
when I was the right kind of kindred brown girl gay or down
to make you look sweet in the eyes of other liberals dipping
their constellations in the same polluted sky, how do you
decide whom to sacrifice and when? Which altar makes you
falter for the father scything others pale as wheat the meet n
greet of your political feat. Dear Optician, turning your wheel
of lenses, I hood: enough! the guff of it stuffing your insecure
belly with the jellied flesh of womb mates bomb mates waving
your MBA in our faces your fascia wax to faeces I mean
bullshit to feed the squid twit digi-inking our fluttering sky,
you fry sister flesh for glory, grab story and photo op co-opt
the co-op hamming for the man, when you could lift us to
another life giving life midwife vs seer turning this green white
winter light to its proper purpose.

Recall another Home

On the Wharf at Brigus

Fill pork rind buckets with squid

32.

Hail Squid Twit full of hate hanging your id out the window
of your belching soul n straight to my digiscreen, you preen
your shit-covered tail fans puce beige and puke grey you
hold up your uglies for the admiration of the smaller squid
twits drinking your brand the white man's abject made object
lobbing the fob only for the basement of your plush tower.
Have your hour hanging snuff porn innocent girls or juliets
julienned and marinated in horse piss as you throw your
weight and administrations nod and sanction. I curse the sick
of it sulphuric reek of rotting blood or brim my eyes plot for
an alternate spot on prime time or fb puffing the guff, purring
the slur of my ruffled feathers chopping buff trolls into egg
rolls deep-fried and sweetened with wing's plum sauce, you
cur I curse you, your thin lip n troll on i'm with stupid's ethic
pathetic as drum roll before the saddest crash of armageddon
generated so money can make itself without us not about
us even the con of economy spins roulette vicious as putin
adoring the ghost of the kgb. Who's free when all systems
interpenetrate as abstraction fucks abstraction and our tender
flesh gets hung out to dry in the dry heat of your thin spirit
thin hair thin atmosphere daring us to push your fragile daddy
one step further. I've had it, mad as a hole digging graves for
gravenstein apples digital light that dapples the scat of feral
cats, bats, squirrels, mammals pooping their biological goo

my guanine your last frontier, fear my spit and puke, my piss and shit, dear Squid Twit, I'll fix you at the crossroads where you saw your god and I saw the stations of our relations I am you as you have fleas and we are all a bother to the purity of the waffle you thought was prick perfect your surfeit of beach party vietnam and the forest rebels have never left us griping and sniping 'til we all fall down, gutter clown, buffoon of the new toupée if only Ru could make you sashay away stay your execution modify your convolutions to shine back your mirror true as achoo! we've had enough of you. If you see your own reflection will you disappear?

Sea wind drenches Saltwater City

        Rises high over Rockies

White sheets Chinook dry

33.

Dear Fido, I tried to be faithful dialing your digital limb mine
hovers six inches beyond the skin electrical and quivering
sensitive as tentacles or the tentative skin of an octopus's
bulbous head mottled with light the wispy blink of thought
hanging material in air for a split before it rushes on I don't
know how to hold the rope of hope through the skin turn
old Chinese lady body wrought different from yogini's bikini
geek muscle still flexible if hexed by the system of brown
and down covered but bothered as birds of bureaucracy
hoover my labour squeeze me tight as good to the last drop of
blood vamping me up to empty. My therapist's avatar draws
boundaries but electric quiver shivers in the cold mists of the
Tao howling for flow or flowers from Hong Kong Artificial
Flower Works #5 and Eliza of riots that sparked our dope oll
i wont is near and fear of freedom not detention centre and
disappear. To break again the already broken mould vs the
Chinese character for home. Security of meat and warm the
killing required for the life of the household trad old but not
only hump it to the monks or sisters Kuan Yin would know
dreaming imaginary meats made of tofu and wheat gluten.
Does tofu faith fake meeting the real deal or is it its own thing
you know like if Ocean Park is as good as Disney? Dizzy in the
spin I wanted to win at the right roulette a bullet or bullion
laying out my meat at market. What's sweet when queer hangs

gender on the winter laundry line? The pat of patriarchy's
taken my hat and I make a run for it hope her something
like a soul's sufficient for the hup of happiness awake in the
styrofoam lunch box as foxes test our spirit's edge seeking
a sign of life. Harm of factory farm, school marm or our
distant Canadarm hold me in your loving or dial that long
distance leave me reeling beneath the glass ceiling my gender
can't bend. I'm dukes up to lash out at the ghost of what was
never there looking as though it were alive oh and cockles
and mussels murder Molly. Solly so solly leave my facial out
of it. Gullible to the circling birds that scream Drop your
hamburger! let go before you know what's yours.

Hot War '67

Heads with black hair scythed and Napalmed

'68 Paris   so what

34.

Dear Scare, I never asked for this straitjacket yellowjacket
buzzing the wasp of your wall nest. We tried to seal you in
with insecticide foam that hardens into a pardon protects
the garden from the wrong cultivation aryan nation or the
flagellating stations of someone else's cross who's boss in
my subaltern hierarchy the hour's power we used to needle
into the soft belly of the man to turn his intestinal worm he
churns but pity's duty steps aside for the ham of compassion
insufficient to the planetary scale of history. You're toast
for the boast that floods the pelvic floor of my vaginal
contractions. The scale of her tender body laid out on brown
dirt. Reverb of wrong pain tears across planet. It's not Trump
Tower babbling nonsense about the middle class while lining
the pocked pockets of Midas men competing with Speedy
muffler trying to duct-tape the rage that gushes, I vomit
planets pulled from inner orbit massive as galactic geology
guts gargantua within. The proper question is how does she
fit my old Chinese lady belly? Your scansion's pentameter can't
magic a gram of my liver's quiver. The angriest woman the
room won't contain institutions' ablutions insufficient
to executive committee's spin on will to expel my hell it gushes
rushes the same lava's river spews rage of all the girls you
swallowed. Hot bile of lady fury vile volcanic melts planetary
demons.

Firm as handshake

Of eager Disdain   can't wait for Palm touch

Grip fingers and squeeze

35.

Dear Civilian, avatar of my racial taming you gush buttery
over the same river ghost who hosts us rinsing the ancient
rocks of history to bring us the water of the future, our
suture's mutual animal spilling past into present through
evaporation condensation, flow of your hydrological cycle as
the others lodged temporary in my watery blood my piss my
spit my vomit and cum the drippy sum of we are all together
commas unsettled by the priority of whose land shaking the
state of real estate or a plate of steak remembering buffalo
rumble flubbed to biting bitter, what cumin can spice this
nightmare? Lucid green of Elbow dreams the body whole
and mobile rush gushing in the hush of what's repressed scan
the land we sampanned from for Old Fish Skin Village or Lai
Chuen the once upon my Shunde home of here we go round
the mulberry fish and fertilizer cycle composing our dykes in
clamouring waves of grain, grown in paddies our legs wet and
leechy up to the knees dreaming water buffalo and a pack of
village dogs tails upcurled on the lookout for bandits tonguing
past dynasties gone wild as feral children escaping through
the gaps in the patriarchy the eye of the emperor dreaming ice
cream. I dream it back to comb my hair black as water of now
speckled white as night descends in clouds of forgetting as
all the twentieth century's wars evaporate. I dream a civilian
Tao unpegged from the call of the colonial remembering not

exactly the wild but the unexpected child of other cultivations
waving not with or against but relations of listening undoing
the buttons of history. Rain on me blood, water or milk liquid
silky as the ilk of connection springs unexpected forms from
the fountain of hope, dope enough to relax all this thinking.

Lo wah kiu Uncle

Wafts up from Tie and spike

Vanishes into hole in mountain

36.

Dear Pluralism, thick fish without history, managing my
difference, finding the soft chair at the unequal table,
squishing your wish for justice. You beat the socks off white
nationalism, I guess. Under your cover, I fail to undermine the
seeming self-evidence my body presents. I dish your platitudes
seeking a door to the core of what's in store, the happy
colonial racing his place while burying the suffering. If the
island's turtles all the way down, what joss can Prospero toss?
Must every mask be gridded to split prairie for subdivision,
the vision of land as perfect commodity supporting the lives
of good Canadian families? My feet long to step off property,
at last touch land. My homily swims a different river. Seeks
to stop the bop. Jackrabbit knives grass hoping to pass a slim
coyote in the night. Or a northern flicker, cheeks streaked and
chest speckled. 'Til then I heckle discontent from the back
of the class, stick data and definition in the gut. Hinge event
to prevent knowledge from accumulating like capital. If this
mama could slap that golden apple back to a barely opened
bud what spud would ground its earthbound ambition? Old
lady wanders barren earth, seeks daughter as heifer long lost
to the economic abattoir as cities gobble children piping
prehistoric amoebae to sea.

What boots click pavement

Signal Arrival at my door

Revolution? or secret police?

37.

Dear Thin King, I sum the heart of your martyrs as horsemen
come steep from steppe raging furious as Genghis Khan. You
howl your waaaaaaaaaaaaaaaaaaaaaa aaaaaaaaaaaaaaaaaaaa of
what deeper than disappointment at the apocalypse galloping
the mare of early-morning wakefulness. Is that light on the
horizon sun or city cranking enlightenment of dead dinosaurs
plus eureka of Edison blinking us awake in the thinning
atmosphere? Dear Prometheus promoting promises you can
never keep working the young men up with the cool of it
while young women take the heat your hero shines still in my
lantern heart drumming the measure of feathers the ick of
Icarus aspiring to summits licking the plumage of plummet
as I eat the plums from the icebox of that sweet Italian tree
in our old yard the one where at night Vancouver's rats ran
afoul of Edward's traps what hap takes its stance on that
damp evening when we totalled our losses like cars running
unexpected lights at busy intersections? Crossroad presents
as crime scene your superhuman power unleashed by accident
the flash of light the crunch of metal see the breaking glass?
I'd prefer to pass in this game of Risk, I lumber I lisp speak
badly into the hell of it.

When I think of you

                    I think of how Thinking

Chinks into bone

38.

Dear Liver, shivering like jelly as the brain takes primacy from
primates mugging the dollar to rough the earth. When I was
a child I thought the soul was a body part lying where you
lie. Are you after all the soul's meat taking heat for what we
denied when we ditched the Tao to go Confucian, Christian,
then Euro Enlightenment Canada Dry? My passions make
corned beef hash of this mess polyvocal syncretic as the
crypt of postmemory's iron box. Am I a butterfly dreaming
I'm awake in the clutter and clamouring for the tidy-up
method? I bang bang on the door loud as chitty and shitty
as the diapers of my future old Chinese lady screaming break
on thru, I've had enough of you. Or are you the box not iron
at all but slippery soft and tender as the octopus's bulbous
head awake in the underwater garden and waving tentacles
beside brain corals contemplating their own convolutions?
Eagle of Prometheus dives deep to peck you. How long before
Ocean Ranger goes down taking the rant and roar of manual
innocents complicit through labour to your watery depths?
You flip and slip your ottery wonder svelte as the pelts taken
by Hudson's Bay as traders drop smallpox blankets up and
down the Northwest Coast. You quiver the tortured magic of
the nightly grow back to push back swell and pulse, even the
eagle's an agent of the arrogant supporting the function of a
dubious god who so loved the world that he gave his one and

only to the homely of our grub and blub flustered in mustard of our own making.

Broken portlight

Hidden hand opens ballast control Valve

Cold ocean massive roll

39.

Dear Lady Madonna, what if the typist was you? Gender
equality of the final violence? Achoo, Maenad Martyr, I
caught you bartering one yellow girl for another, mangling
your metaphor for spaghetti dreaming of wonton mein. Why
not choose the cute one the fun n feisty one n leave the meek
and geek to howl outside the door? When he hired me was
that a one-up on your ass? I guess it was, twisted sister of my
leaking blister. I guess I'm sorry, but you sure got me back
good. Go ahead, steal my clothes, the black dress with brass
buttons, long out of style now in the how of your cowabunga,
I bought that one in the Plum of aspiration, middle of skid
road industrial Vancouver dreaming Miami Vice, Los Angeles
or anarchic UK our Vander Slime not nearly romantic sinister
as Thatcher. Sheena the punk rocker can't be an Asian of
any persuasion. Don't you know they skin us the same way?
But I typed your lie, got expelled from the collective, here
let's talk about that tall glass of beer break the fourth wall of
our political correlative and call our cousins home. I hang
my competitive teenage asshole out the window of my soul.
My brass bowl's gone cold ringing for the bodhisattva of my
generation's haptic wired on Starbucks and here we are now
entertain us to the mirror pool of our own self-obsessed
drownings. Fuck Oleanna if the white man can't drop his
mirror either. My waffle's starved for eggs n syrup the stirrup

of giddyap n git along little digger, Holy Madonna at the corner advertising your West Coast cool. You fool, it's only teenaged waste a taste of the hate already spun for us in the sick of our own Confucian patriarchy in exile the barter of the village lane begging one girl to marry handsome while the other's fodder for bandits to slit gut ditch by the roadside. Rancid roar of lady revenge congealing jealousy for the sad and had. Dear Duck, because I don't want her to see me with you, I leave my trust to your daddy's over-healthy fund. Let's talk Wu Tsao gouging the eyes of rivals, chopping their arms and legs off and dropping them in vats of hot oil labelled pig for stigma, who needs the cargo of colonialism when sisters can do it for themselves?

It is beautiful

                    I didn't make it

I want to break it

40.

Dear Gelatinous Disc, swimming between L4 and L5 wishing
you were a jellyfish dreaming she is a man, did you think this
body was an ocean or did you just get tired of holding up
the world? You and me, we tumbled crooked from the dark
cave of mother's unspeakable. Old Dr Ross said after thirty,
so I guess we're not doing too bad in the Glad garbage bag of
history making a run at the yellow light, time's tight I sight the
Story of tokyo rose in the over-bright headlights of the new
suvs blinding me with science. Or prescience, the precinct
of the body as cop singing we had it all but now it's time to
pay. What would you say to holding the tide a little longer as
this asian dances the conga line of get us there collectively or
not at all, while the arch of patriarchy still elevates the lovely
dropping tokens into the ancient fare box TTC to YYC while
glowworms swing digital and greedy brothers grab every
scrap they can get from the colony of this body. Burden of
representation Ruptures your fourth wall and you get on my
nerves sciatic sclerotic bursting the bubble of my upright
citizen. Turns out we came through the door of aftermath
our plumbline glum receiving what's left after the Sum of the
Heart's been tallied, reckoning the bill of my disposable soul.
I slam the bowl of rice worried there might not be another,
post mem the korean Embargo that shut HK from china made
the debt personal as if you starved me out yourself. If there's

enough pretty stuff, will you forget your sorrow, return as
sandwich meat for vertebra to give me my day in the curt
court of just us? Or stay busted and let the temple crumble
bombed, embargoed, shunned and silenced, then suddenly
raised up as quota neolib commodity for the oddity of taking
our place in overdetermined space not the final frontier but
the rear-view mirror, leg cast like jimmy stewart spinning
conspiracy theories n watching the world go by.

Left foot warrior one

          Basement of Bauhaus Tower

Such a poser

41.

Dear Racial Representation, clerk of exhaustion splashing
ads for my services over the cover of every grant application,
make sure you buy me cheap. Show me the toilet of my
failure to deliver, as your co-op already showed me the
cesspool of cessation, I shiver swim between the how of hot
chinese money still in the hands of the chinese Man parking
his porsche for the triple occupation, bombing, rape and
embargo that's the cargo of Psyche seeking her lover under
cover of four impossible tasks. Thank you for my second-hand
classical education full of holes n reeking of naphthalene.
Your mothballs scent their desire to cling to completeness
violated in another iron box, the crypt of postmemory
occupies my liver to push the time of my spine out of joint.
I howl mournful at the door of love my clumsy hands sort
seeds stitch skins torn across continents by the hellish greed
of capital. That apple red hot as the video shop bombed by
the Squamish Five outraged in the cage of bad narratives.
What if the apple finds pleasure in being bought and sold? My
avatar swallows sedatives and beta blockers awake to chemical
emotions lotioned by the grease of designated cash. I halve
my mask to spin flesh off spine, go offline to return weather
to ether mutter my mother back into being. My hot proxy
teeth bite your Cold War economics. My sorrow's haptic
simulacrum returns as massive RAM the glistening fleece

of my wolf in designer clothing. No wet suit's sufficient for the polluted river twice, as the golems of oligarchy double your trouble signify coming as going appropriation as apology repositioning the nation as old power in new shoes. Butterfly bails on beauty as the colonial division of intimacy bums my balm. We scream for face cream as if any potion could make the motion unsettle Robert remake rules as roots finally too deep for school.

Congratulations you've

Arrived at Arrivals

Gate of my open business

42.

Dear Wolf in Deer's Clothing, what loathing do you suffer
unjustly? Every dog should have its play, hanging kong's
continuity with catch, while you hatch nature as continuous
with human. What do ruminants owe you anyway? A patch
of grass, a last to make the shoe fit? Or a first for the burst of
beauty you embody: the quiet, padding Wisdom of one who
likes the taste of meat. Your pelt's svelte, hairs sensitive as
breeze in rushes, surely you have a right to the Occasional
sheep we count trying to sleep while our investments follow
the whim of the market. Human dreams would be overrun
without you. This finite earth needs dearth to live. What
gives? I sheath my shiv to wash your pass, while you watch for
weakness, target the gull as your duty to cull. You leap against
the odds of guns, shepherds, domestic cousins cowards who
have prematurely surrendered the species to man. What a
jam. If I call you Chance, would you dance, or roll the dice,
old grey-eyed prince of banter, cantering with ungulates
against the glut of bulls at market, stark as was or were, your
subjunctive eyes dreaming of butterfly effects, shaking men
from High Places halfway across the world?

reading Instructions

cap kHarLaMoV in kNee

for justifying margins

43.

Dear Listener, glistening sad and had on the stairway to
heaven. You shine wet as the spit levered your way by
ascending lovers. The snot of your allergic reaction dribbles
nostril to lip why won't you wipe? Kleenex's best customer
metes out sheets conscious of old growth cut for asswipe,
Hallmark, corrugated cardboard and your beloved books.
You couldn't score without paper, the door of your doggy
dip n soggy sip sobbing for the FOB while lucky bullies lob
eggs your way. Sunny side up or over easy the greasy tease
isn't innocent singing the pitch to make your nose bleed.
Don't plead, it makes matters worse, the grim curse of your
saltwater journey blighted in nightmares of fresh off the flight
the same blue and purple striped sweater twice, three times,
four, why wear anything else and why bother washing when
you could disappear into the sour sweat smell of tomorrow's
sorrow same as yesterday's and today's? Wanna play see see
my playmate stalemate as in forget it you reek the germs of
harm the terms of the tarmac god's her own father and she
don't even believe in him. Later, other's cooties the tormented
sad boy sketches graffiti cocks into hairy pussies on the backs
of bathroom doors. Fills the hat she lent you with rocks
and hurls it across playground or Alexandra in Language
Arts pinches your arm hard as she can the searing pain of it
scream and shame or hush now and pretend the arm's not

yours. Score of he dresses well I'm sure it's okay. Translate to
Humiliation's on and on and on, keep on rockin' baby. What
balm could beautify this appointment, when the Queen of
Exile's still a queen stolen because some hellish headbanger
saw the object he could make her? Beg her for the secret oil
of your toil's completion, psyched in the night by the
blooming flower of once upon the gorgon your banishment
from presence dissolved in the how of history's now the Genie
of Genealogy leaking logic's heavy water, it's fine you bide your
time but which time jointing the river for the dam's sticking
point, her ointments oink with bores who were men turned
to stone by the skin deep swinging its own fragile power fine
as powder and temporary but still not yours. In the corridor
of this war, DO NOT ENTER sign abandons all faith as even
wraiths dissolve in the hiss of this the dampest mist.

Winter Dinner

                    North Atlantic shore

Pease pudding   salt beef   cod's kiss

44.

Dear Queen of Exile, I sunk my river to try your door, the
scoreboard's sore at halftime running your football to the
het net the pet's bet gambling on horsemen wishing you'd
finally call an end to it all. Don't stall, the driving force of
the revolution's already eaten, apple is dying to sell the
temporary measure as final product. Your lotion's deepest
emotion holds subaltern beauty to subterranean standards
get it on hansard plant me an answer before the ding ding
of springtime releases you back to mama. My boomer's lurgy
as clergy splurging on the uber of Alice's magic mushroom,
terse as douchebags restraining urges from the nonchalant
wells of their own repressions. Butter me with the essence of
every flower and leaf, cover my grief with the Asian substitute
for the pink, the lily and the blooming rose, the winter juices
of every summer beauty on duty for death advertising cars,
phones, social networks or routers for sad sacks dreaming
eternal sunshine. Mask me to grasp everlasting love, my cover
for help from above or the rough justice meant for some other
brother in the submarine of limbo arms akimbo indignant
about the dog's every biscuit. Truth is, for all my bravado,
I won't brave your door. Your beauty's too terrible, and
I'm fried in the terror my mama can't turn the seasons to
guarantee my safe return. Maenad Martyr rages at the edge
of it, oh holy Stephanie, I flail narcotics of narcissus, my

desire for you is not a nice desire, here's a flower for Saint Iris, her live horses the latest casualty of Nanking.

$39.99 at Sephora

BB cream on sale

Precious poppy pink

45.

Dear Uncle, the other Little Boy, dead before she was born,
what horn gored you? Neglect as Grandmother partied to
numb the rain? Or were you the child on the bayonet, baying
hound the horsemen will never catch? I was so unhappy
then, I'm happy now, I don't want to talk about it. I stalk her
balk, sinister ghost awake in its iron blood. I mask, I hood,
avatar of Freud, dreaming traumatic contents. If I pull truth's
tooth from crypt, decode the Japanese message, will you set
me free? Lift the curse of Saint Stephen getting even with
the colonizer by ripping open Chinese bodies, sexing the
rap of rape the women vs murder the men herded south for
point-blank executions. Women stacked for hacking bayonet
hatchet cock and sear the meat we eat while looking neat.
Unspeakable in the house of cure, surefire wit of chinese
japanese dirty knees money money money money, forgot
your manners cheese your please. Prick props propaganda
as goose forgets fork on right and knife on left or the other
way around? Grandfather chops her cheongsams and I dream
Saint Iris storming Stephanie's door, the core of her maenad
beautiful virginal channel of change. I rampage, bite the hand
of the man, cram a gram of whatever I'm branded banging the
door I can't or won't open. That cornucopia of Chinese horror
reeking of mothballs and feasting on delicious beasts to forget
the Confucian way. What if the answer can't be documented

on shame's train? If no mucus could prove this? Every dollar restores honour. The child I never had rides my back hissing sweetly to egg me on.

If Scene's a meme team

                 Venus Transiting Virgo

Avid birder threads spiderweb

46.

Dear Fish, I drew you wet slippery from the ghost river, flip
flap of your meaty body sudden flesh caught in the mesh of
my mare dreaming horses and water courses the go and flow
of we are all together measures of weather banging drums
our thumbs tucked tight into fists of protection rejection the
captain of whose ship quipping like an Englishman for a better
colonialism while broken boatmen stoned on opium smoke
visions of rest. Escape from the go go go of the go-down the
lowdown on the cargo he stored there before the bombing.
I don't want to talk about it, I suffered so you don't have to,
why go digging for the antimatter I hid to protect you? Saint
Iris looks back at the horror and turns to stone. Don't dial
that waste seek grace a place for yellow the racing pulse of
propulsion always go go going to the go go frivolous as disco
dancing to die another day. The new bullies see your dance
smirk privilege you must be rich if you can shine like that.
Maenad Martyr thins her grin sapping to sob me too but her
two rages in the reverb burning bio or blurb as though five
minutes of fame could boil a whole pot of soup. We group
our crabs crawling to haul another one down and another one
down the brown drain of we could be dancing glancing like
princes in the nonce of dunces munching shit in the classroom
where the revolution's new suit glibs if your pain's real then
shut it. Maenad's gutted mutters her reverb soft as guilt not

guilt stunted in search for words, you heard me, bard's only for dialectic tragic as Butterfly dreaming the future as one fine day.

Winnipeg Grenadiers defend

        Christmas Day   Wan Chai Gap

Michif whispers lift sibylant on mountain breeze

47.

Dear Revolution, enhancing your chance for the Cleanest
Hands rise and rinse me on the inside flesh of my flesh and
bone of my bone. You hone me cut for the sharpest diamond
dogging the hog of my best meat-eating days. Praise the naked
suffragette her longing for Park Lane the glass tower of her
vindication. She wants her cheongsam back, not the Japanese
soldier. Put the scissors back in Grandfather's hands, redress
the dress, put the baby back in the cradle and send the soldiers
back to Hirohito. Restore their innocence and make their
smooth skin shine again, give them back to their mamas to
raise them right. Refuse the white man's modernity. Send him
back down the long arc of his land and spirit troubles. Return
him to eden to renegotiate with his one god the relation
between body and mind. Dream a different dry martini how
the rev of another engine might feed our Weather together
raining for a new romance.

Astronaut Salary

        Stubs Toe   on first world problems

Roughs glum on roomba

48.

Dear Pork, turning the tines of the time's tithes activating
the histamines of history, i'm blustery feeding the fluster of
eat vs breathe dense weave of needs warped in the woof of
guard dogs or hell hounds while your cerberus munches
tariffs. Even to enter hell ain't easy. Dear Pig-Beneath-Roof,
sighing for eternal spring, holding off the autumnal spectre
of slaughter, the gotcha of what you ate before reading the fine
print ingredient list required by the Canadian Food Inspection
Agency. Dear Dogma, I'm switching my digits, ditching my
ideological fidget for the fudge of muddy vision the quick
incision that cuts my banana umbrella. Hey Fella, can that
tear gas the fear of near gas gathering passes for every fry
swimming the same river, fish eluding crowd control to school
the dialectic's communist credentials.

Cookie monster blue

      Workshop dreams all sailors free

Market boxes   pork rind crisp

49.

Dear Pigeon, passing judgment on herders and murderers
lining pockets with death. I flop to your posture the gesture of
elvis after achilles abandoned his post least or most dancing
the bird sage all chest and hip skipping the dip of sitting.
Come the revolution, I'll be the first one shot for not toeing
the pigeon's line of flight, path of proper left or right in tighty-
whities humming the hum of ham. My hawk's heart lost as
tonal ghost bombed out of mother tongue still swinging the
door for the mock of democracy vs left foot kicks as prick's
mayhem and murder of whatever goat's got today's tongue, my
pidgin carries messages over broken glass and shot to back of
head all the long coast of the south china sea spanning the silk
road of my asian continuum, hum for your life from amitabha
to om mani pedi away across the multiverse of a child's garden
only pardoned in the England of mockery's '97 retreat as river
gushes '67's headless body after headless body of revolution in
crisis vomiting citizens in a fit of self-loathing by comparison
in the false mirror of euro-cap's god crisis. Did you ever dream
your falcon could fly so far? Rumble the reverb of my teenage
asshole hanging competition resentment out guilt's golden
window to fumble the grumble low as sad and had and nuclear
as the trail of Marie remembering burning vision Great Bear
Lake to Hiroshima or Nadine recalling toxic tailings Kirkvine
to Kitimat the hard hunt of money as virus kicks Osiris and

my grandma pulls out her sewing box and stitches and stitches
and stitches.

From Giant Mart like the other kids

         At Our Lady of Lourdes

I wanted   the blue uniform

50.

Dear Fragrant Harbour, welcome the headless bodies of my
great-uncles, -aunts and -cousins, rice field farmers, peasant
workers, capitalist roaders of the revolutionary apocalypse
ditzing down the Pearl River after a shot to the back of
the skull and a good beheading, welcome to the horror of
knowing only Uncle Eight as numbers One, Two, Three, Four,
Five and lucky Seven go to heaven or smoke that last cigarette
before the final number we slumber in the paths of capital
pray money will make up for all that's gone funny i mean
not ha ha but funny strangelove learning to love the bomb
swinging from the hang seng star of my burnt-out metaphor
burnt-out semaphore signalling darlin' can't you hear me, sos.
Dear Japanese Imperial army, I know what you did. They only
chased her round the dining table, spinning the lazy Susan
one delicious dish for every child and we'll never go hungry.
Chased her round the dining table, my life's so good now
it was terrible then why would I want to talk about it shout
about it pout about it, or the son who died, one ideology for
every id seeking a coherent position to hang your subject on,
win the spin twirl of you are what you eat and what are you
suturing? She sews and sews and sews when she can afford
the fabric her tiny nimble hands stitching to fit every curve
for the mah-jong table of forgetting, high colour, tiny snaps,
shimmering patterned fabric. Grandfather's handsome tennis

elbow loses advantage from the nearly even-Steven deuce of
his new-style kung fu, hits the ball and hits the ball and hits
the ball as if enough smashes could make me bright immune
I'll sing that tune holding out for a hero when your tennis
whites at zero even if you put a whole lifetime in at the club
you flub it then dub it in English can't escape the crude of
my mother tongue flapping nonsense in the wind. Shut up
shut up we don't speak these things let's sugar plum fairy and
dairy farm it cover it over with dust from the wind. She sews
and sews and sews for prestige, and the shop makes enough
money for everyone to gather round the roundabout, eat
swimming shrimp and fatty pork and all the little dumplings,
tight and close or hard and fast. Dear Ha Gow, Dear Siu Mai,
I sigh for all the not saying. He hit the ball and hit the
ball soon his serve smashed all other serves as he cleaned
up on court. Let's go see The Nutcracker my unspeaking
granddaughter whose tongue is white as snow, and leave him
at home who cares about him, I'm so happy now I have you.
Don't ask me about it, let's go to Park Lane all clean marble,
I'll buy you a dress some shoes a car we're richer than them
now and I can't ask more than that. I don't know how to ask,
if none of this had happened, I wouldn't have you.

Better than a Japanese soldier, you.

Better than a bayonet, you.

Better than the dining table, you.

Better than a lazy Susan, you.

Better than my dead eldest son, you.

Better than a beautiful cheongsam, you.

Better than swimming shrimp, you.

Better than Dairy Farm strawberry ice cream, you.

Better than a Slazenger racquet, you.

Better than Martina Navratilova, you.

Better than a smash serve ace, you.

Better than the Sugar Plum Fairy, you.

Better than Park Lane, you.

Oh, make a lot of money, buy a fancy car, build a skyscraper, swing from a star.

Hark the dogs doggy

Do doldrums in the midnight hour

Mud paddles subject

51.

Dear Oolong, if there were no such thing as tea, none of this would have Happened. Bo nay, gook bo, heung pin, lung ching or ti gwoon yum, I hum, infusions a solution to remaining alert to irony, as sleepers puff opium trading the doozy of drowsiness for the carrot of charity draining the Oort cloud of our distant origins. Alert in the iron box, tempest teases schoolyard bullies flipping their hair like Farrah. Mine's too flat to feather, birds gather in conferences unable to backcomb for the stand-up comedian or punk rock pork hock. My dialect ditzes for the foetal leaf unfurling in hot water as English breakfast, Russian Caravan, Prince of Wales or Earl and Lady Grey. I hack for smack, heroin, morphine or crack as Jardine Matheson plies the China trade, pirating porcelain, silk, cotton and tea, items of use traded for the inducement of rest. That's okay, I'll dream my way back into your loving arms race, Cold War or trade war parading handbags from Prada, Coach and Chanel as students toss Molotov cocktails against tear gas on the MTR. Our scars glisten bright as stars fishing for birds in the Silver River a sliver of memory flashing light on our addictions enforced by gunboat diplomacy while geomancers crack ox scapulae for a route out of psychic unrest. What mettle could test this, gunpowder green or Iron Goddess, as my fireworks go up in smoke? I poke for a new

Berlin, find a cross on the road as fentanyl crisis boom echoes across centuries of artificial sleep.

Perturbed galaxy ejects

                        Tidal stream of stars

River jumps fish

52.

Dear Silence, travelling as a Kind of Love, you protect the innocent from the injuries of the harmed, alarmed by violation the heart can't count. What the soldier did to her, I was so unhappy then, if I tell you it will be as though I let him cut you too. I don't want to wield that knife, the strife of repetition confirming my perdition. Dear Cut, Dear Beheading, Dear Ten Thousand Women, what Iris witnessed killed her. The Old Ones don't know the talking cure, what if my therapist's avatar doesn't work on the people of Tang Street the ones who crossed the mountains leaving their dynasty a thousand years behind? What if it's only for one god cultures of confession, the absent present people of the on/off switch, and the lesson of my species leaves me in the dirt? For folks who ching circular on the how of tao, what's left after I tell? I blink in the zero/one of the whole and broken line. If I speak my Hush what world will whirl back to me? Will ten thousand flowers bloom or will the violets of violence boom me back to a jar of hot oil, without arms, without legs, without eyes, sightless pig of obliteration sunk and scalded in hatred's imagination deep as the lurch of my tentative love the one I don't dare lest it bind you too? It's better to be Canadian dance The Nutcracker of ballerina beauty white as an Eastern snowstorm so close you can't see your hand.

Woman emperor

Intrigue by North Star

Align spine to crack back

53.

Dear Witness Protection with a predilection for memory
without form. I swarm collect like flies on a stagnant pond
or floodplain naming the gain of my silence by holding off
the hot gush of feeling. I deal the cards of sharks gambling
on the beauty of buildings, architectures of glass and steel
the pristine elegance of the perfect boardroom. My class is
cover for the gashes of the past. Ten thousand women burn
their eyes out polish mirrors of touchpads and smartphones,
prod circuits beneath microscopes with tweezers too tiny for
eyebrows arching surprise at innovative horror. If the lurk of
work could perk a new army of the damned crammed in facts
and farms alarmed and clocked to ramp production, it's no
mistake that money is paper covering the drapes of our lapses.
We burn a spirit version for the ones who took their silence
with them, cars, shirts, palaces of gold, computers, cellphones,
eyeglasses and billfolds, the cold hard cash of a smoke that
knows no other hold.

Empire flops digital

                             Manual labour

Extends secret handshake

54.

Dear Say without Saying, Dear Role without Playing,
flaying flesh off the back of my therapist's avatar halving
the quest of my pluralist's samovar, what if I'm cured in my
Western regions while the Eastern lesion deepens? If I bleep
the expectation of production to survive the occupation that
ended eighty years ago, will you return the village we fled
screaming? Turn the clock back to watchtower and banditry
while I thread the cycle of silkworms fed by mulberry leaves
nourished by carp crap feeding mulberry bushes? I eat or
sell the fish. My nimble fingers twine fine lines, spin a win
for the export market. Is there any going back or does my
wheel churn a different return? One that spurns payback for
the kerning of yearning, turns seasoning for steak and waits
for the bake of the warming earth? Is Old Fish Skin Village a
double for Lai Chuen, or is the refrigerator factory the true
cool of what was razed in China's modern stern the burn of
my Shunde home? My inner critter stutters on human, seeks
language for fur and down, mysterious bacteria swimming
the distance of my interior rivers, quivering lively as hives
buzzing the swarm of another collective suggesting the harm
of another invective, listing ships for yet another quip.

Cry havoc!

and let Slip

the dogs of autobiography

55.

Dear Bodhisattva, our administration denies your application
requests further documentation on the relations of your
emanations rendering dubious the station of your creation.
We need fists to prove this. We need fish, we need bones, a
pound of mesh, the behest of the donor laying kroner on the
holler of your partial dollar. We need fodder for our error.
We'll take your tribute, your mother, your father, a grist of
sisters and your heart and liver to luck our buck, clean the
hands of our boys their pleasures and ploys are the first ducks
in our row. Your attitude of beatitude belies ingratitude to
the ones who died for the sins they pinned on you. Blue?
Achoo! Your allergy's a cover for the coven roasting witches
we hunted to make the world spin the other way round. Have
your say. We'll listen to the first sentence substituting every
noun for a clown in brown makeup, take up every connotation
for our own elation. The conflagration won't talk about a
past that doesn't serve it soft as a futon for our loft or ice
cream at the takeout with strawberry sauce. Lay your lubber
on the tracks of the hack cracking codes to keep what we
have under wraps. We'll stack your vertebrae backwards to
slow your cerebral progress through dense biscuits of empty
carbs, while we lark on a wing of our own narking, build more
parking for CEOs and fund managers while you bandage what's
bleeding. We gotta keep on feeding, it's how we're leading in

the polls for trolls. Stow your eggroll 'til you've grown more
bean sprouts, grouted the wall we've built to keep you out
and double-glazed the glass ceiling. Once more, with feeling!
We want you reeling the bludgeon of fake news 'til the truth
makes you stupid, caught in the loop of chasing the tail we
pinned on your donkey. Had enough? You're through? Here's
a revolving door to take your exit, all the world's a gauge
of how we'll measure you by a yardstick turned to beepers
doubling down on the best bloopers we lifted from the
stone of your phone. Don't groan, your loan's overdue and
accumulating interest in the algorithm of our decision, baking
lesions deep in the meat of your liver. We'll peck it out for
you at a good price, calculated in rice, be nice and we'll throw
in an eagle for free.

Sister Rita

                         Hawks a gob

Scoffs at toffs   sips duck congee

56.

Dear Secret Santa, huffing the bluff of the big reveal stealing
the squeal of negative space, I grace this race with a kind of
hush the grave trace of what was stubbornly never spoken, to
heal this deal feel the scream reeling the real unreal as though
what you see under the light is actually evidence as providence
manifest flat as a patty cake quick-fixing the surface not
preventing the ghost river rushing beneath. As though you
could hold it and own it. Stone and debone it, unthrone it,
cone it, loan it to ebook readers for fast grab of watch it. Allot
me a sour hour, grey dark glower of thick beasts slinking
slow through mist. Hiss of this mothball grief that returns all
presents taken as liquid nitrogen cooling our ancient scars to
scatter fish among stars swimming against the constellations
that look the same for millennia despite the speed of light. I'm
on a night flight swimming the underwater sky the full fathom
of can't take it back and can't see it either. Here's a residue,
triple occupation as station of my grim asian hum dimming
the lights to find the truth of all that transpired after our
brothers un-ned us, I was so unhappy then, I'm happy now,
why would I want to remember? The secrets of Chinatown are
no secrets at all, ancient or otherwise, when subject's a split
slit bleeding in the dark.

Second-gen Egg Sacrifice

Nascent memory

Blunders through bloodstream

57.

Dear Dirty Knees, flipping your uniform at deep inside we're
all the same, my brain drain claims your Toilet Brush's shitty
equivalences hovering at the box office of universal pictures.
Between frankly my dear and merry christmas mr lawrence we
travel belt and road to arabia chanting Om or give me a Home
on the same thin breath dicing difference between chinese
and japanese. While buffalo dream swarm intelligence no
soldiers can solder the four winds. I learned love for the indiv
anyway, sort the stash between fame game and community
chest, puffing my pidgin to line the widget's hardscrabble
interior. Raw or cooked my fish dishes the dialectic seeking
adjacencies of water. Who's slaughtered turtle island vs
Asian continent shifts the drift of plates and teacups. Sigh of
scythes, debts of death too deep for the treasons of reason or
pangaea's distant relations turtle shell's moves grooves cracks
and hacks. My bodhisattva dangles miracles in binary code,
Broken and Unbroken lines signal tumble of yarrow as good
for digestion. How sings the jay in the swing between imperial
and canadian? Can't the see of saw prognosticate the suffix
of suffering? Prick of thumbs skims terrible pathos in all that
Iris witnessed, while the nuclear option skinned generations
of real human flesh against the metaphor of race. We swing
retribution on trauma's glittering chandelier, every bump a
different bead refracting the hiss of history splashed across
specific windows.

Wash Body   Stitch Story

        Hot Brand Cracks shell

Ghost turtle dives   ocean divides

58.

Dear Echo Chamber, the difference between Japanese Imperial
and Japanese Canadian swims an ocean, pacific's specific
as the frump in lumpen. Old Owl asks: "Do you care more
for Chinese people or Japanese people?" What cracks your
convolutions between soldier and internee? That summer
Monika and I drove in my red Nissan Sentra echoing the
red Datsun Mom and Dad had when we first moved to
Newfoundland, this trip Calgary to New Denver. "Gardens
are thus not so much invented as always erupting from the
difference of gardeners and the traces of other forces at work
in their midst." What can sprout in the garden after the arrival
of the secret police? Can there be poetry after New Denver?
The soul of the situation busts my gut. What spurn could
I return? The split unbridgeable of those branded enemy
alien vs "Perhaps when we were raping her we looked at her
as a woman, but when we killed her we thought of her as
something like a pig." King Kong touches Hong Kong and
his sad gorilla hand cradles the screaming lady. Even CIBC
can't put Canadian beside Imperial without getting squirrelly.
The nut of nation cracks eggs instead, as though omelette
were substitute for meat. What comes first, the magic or
the nation? As old Anderson wobbles Hans Christian or
Benedict? Swing latinate to ling what this flesh can't pass, as
current fascisms remember the same sorrow to call me "back"

under cover of another wounded brother. Can't have it out on twitter as Echo flits from circuit to circus, rages from body to machine to body to dream seeking the feather coat shed as flesh hoping she could leave it by the mirror pool just long enough to get clean.

Clear pool reflects bright

    Eye   dreams white flower fading

Touch pad to wash face

59.

Dear Pool, only for you I doff my feather dress, swan
sings sadly to lake, already ballerina thin on the verge of
disappearance. Will you mourn me when I'm clean? I shed
flesh dreaming of princes who won't split the cheque.
Dreaming of other swans. What bill does the one who spies
buy? When the hunter looks, is it me or his own image he
seeks? Does he dream becoming pure as the hunted, long
for the dogs who lick his hands instead to shred him, release
him from his own private emperor? Or does he want my
disappearance so he too can peloton the pool, contemplate
his rugged individual, reach out to grasp his own forgotten
beauty? My hands swing digital before the last part of me
vanishes into ether. I flit tree to rock, mainframe to brain
drain seeking to say back the code to release trauma's
treasure. I measure. Have I stated my case, laid waste to ducks
unlimited clamouring to get in the right row for the right
show? I retweet, remember massive wings that arched open
to sky. Now, satellites circle higher than my line of flight, dish
the deal fast as data, spin the whirl of dizzy planets unwinding
death to dance. Do you hear me in the circuits calling out
my love? Or only the hounds, moon-starved, ravenous and
confused over who's their daddy? All those colour-blind
soldiers I nursed in my white uniform. I storm, I mourn,
screech my owl into gale force wind.

You dim duck

To love the single swan is already

Surrender to the dying corps

60.

Dear Pentheus, I didn't mean to make you and Actaeon go
Dutch. What's Greek to you is Chinese to me. A fool, I flee,
wanting to dodge the hard hit of the murder ball but evading
responsibility instead. If all balls were mirrored could all
kisses taste like honey? Instigating revolution I still chase
the money, hot Asian or vacation, someone's gotta stock the
cupboard and have fun doing it. I'm bopping for shopping.
Ramen, guns, computers or meat buns, what matter feeds or
greases the track of how do we get there from here? Squid
Twit leverages fear, while the rear guard poses avant la lettre,
scrambling for language after they've already eaten the cake.
What stakes when the principles of carnival are dubious on
the feminine? I twine my vines, the double thread, knotted
at one end and sharp at the other, no one asked the snake
about the sensation of swallowing its own tail. I'd advise you
to drink the wine. Is there so much hate for the ones we love?
Kate's hounds howl the sick sound of rebound, as dogs devour
masters and mothers massacre, mistaking children for beasts.
How can a king know which troublemakers are holy? Is it
possible to become and recover mother by dancing with her?
When the law sticks in every sovereign's craw, what subaltern
gesture can rupture into agency? Must the flesh absorb the
armour to render the body safe? Or are our bones already
glittery on the inside striding us wide into being?

Butterfly hums Tennessee waltz

Best Friend and Sweetheart flutter nostalgic

Wings of monarch unfold

61.

Dear Dialectic, I duck your draft when your north wind
blows too cool for school. When your protestant gets feisty
about property howls hard work and sign the petition, I get
skittish except in times when I can't bake the stakes. When
land teacher gifts ritual I commit to tao for now. My i ching
won't turn you away at the door since to refuse you would
be to let you in. I spin roulette to get the hang of yin or yang,
whip through zarathustra to push beyond evel knievel. As
daredevil lays chips on 0 or 1, I dim the skim and praise the
circle, old Turtle Shell that contains many binaries in sets of
3 and 6, cycling young yin to old yang and back the other way,
spirals snail shell or galaxy, strands of DNA. What say? When
history hisses under conditions not of my choosing, I cruise
for a purging, lose my Cultural Revolution to the arbitrary
mystery of who lives and who dies while smashing the Four
Olds. No one said the circle always swings peaceful. I toss
pre-revolution cash to lay lines open and closed. When the
gram says "skinning" I close my eyes and welcome the hex.
The Lady of Fate emerges.

Fire in the lake

Banishes cause for sorrow

Stretches animal skin over branches   horns attached

62.

Dear Sister, if you look in the mirror and see your Typist,
step away from the mirror. The reflection is real. The glass is
about to shatter. Door deer in the headlights, there is no break
on through for anyone who bleeds. Shift sideways to ground
before he catches you in his glass eye and every shard flies out,
gores you in the tender parts, takes you, takes me, takes the
entire army of the harmed. Dear Medium of Medusa loosing
your fury to the scurry of worry, it's how the shudder gets
you, buttering the wrong guttural, stuttering for the machine
gun because clear speech has already been co-opted in the
sold-out co-op scrambling for language after the truth has
been gutted down to its sweetest entrail. The war isn't over.
When the rage of the cut one shatters glass stuck for staring
the how of the tao sips indirection. We sisters are barely
mothers, virgin surrogates of the fertile, remaining upright
on the ruin of earth. I'm still tempted by the commodities
of god, not exempted from complicity in capital. I've been
unhomed by the pidgin, ditched in the margin account of the
scouts who came converting, blurting for the dialectic of the
One, that stun of a gun blundering powder for muskets while
privateering rockets to the final frontier. Perseus wants you to
see yourself in him, to see the true horror of the gorgon you've
claimed in pain. What if she's beside you, solid as a clock,
leaking time for a dime, parsley, sage, a female rhyme?

Snake lady slips Sideways

To yellow river

Wet mud of Tong Yan's birth

63.

Dear Chinese Lady, awake in your takeout box, I staked your
place with finger lace, detective of inhabitation. I hucked
my hakka great-grandma a hawker's history though she was
matriarch of the village happy valley before the british. Get
martial when your history's partial. I star my lover's crossed
path for the cowherd's hum of heterosexuality as weaver
strokes weft to avoid warp's war. I trounce my subject's
pounce 'til the crack fracks in a different direction. North by
northwest or northeast the least of my geese works her way
south for the winter. Every weaver needs sisters to constellate
her cosmos. Dear Vega, your URL's gone vegan, pining for
Tegan and Sara, your proper position in the mission of
direction leading the coalition from persecution, locuting your
location loquaciously as loquats at lunar new year listening
for another orientation to time. The takers masquerading as
givers know exactly who they are. Slowly, the earth shifts her
axis. In the Year 13,727 you'll return to your ancient glory,
streaming a river of geese or magpies, squawk chatting the
beauty of feathers iridescent blue and green.

A Lyr hacks songbird

            Measures distance to Sun

Helium giggles time zone shift

64.

Dear Tao, old rotary, turtle shell squeal whistling in flames to name the hell of a revolutionary god, I split my cod debone at spine to line a whispered history, astronaut's impossible labour climbs back down millennia, returns to earth. The i of ching blusters to shang ancestry, priestess geomancer of a bad romance. I'll take a chance on democracy from below glowing in the slow heat of another ember. Guilt shines beneath quilt of magpies flashing shimmery feathers as protestant lies down on her bed of nails, dials dialectic for that long-distance feeling, beguiled by the gush of blood staining the shroud of her own making. What king could ding this, melt dragons in cauldrons to brew a better soup? I stoop, regroup, loop Yue for Tin Hau, Gwoon Yum for Ocean Goers, Avalokiteśvara of the Long March Across Deserts, Bodhisattva of Water, Queen Mother of a Different West, rescues father and brothers from massive spiral sea to sky storm. Now, her incense coil burns above, snakes from ceiling of wet temple, steps from station of the cross. We were not yet Chinese when Shang was ancient. I dream my being returned to Weaver's once and future North Star. Dear Tong Yan, I pilot my ship on South China Sea, blink my split toenail, cast net for wishes, bungle my smuggle for a pot of rice steamed with salted fish.

Echo wagers cap against standard

     cues Pool table to return Love's body

in Remembered Alphabet's lunar pull

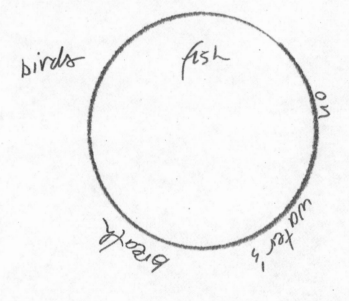

birds

fish

on

water's

birch

fish

exhales

dissolved

air

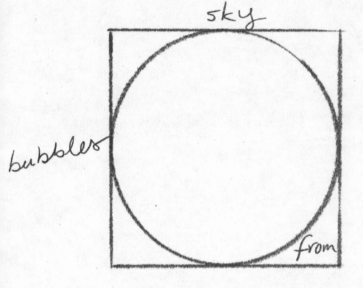

Sources/Voices/Inspirations

20.   "Egg black and green": Grateful acknowledgment
to Winston C. Kam for his story "Inside the Black
Egg," originally published in *Many-Mouthed Birds:
Contemporary Writings by Chinese Canadians*, ed.
Bennett Lee and Jim Wong-Chu (Vancouver: Douglas
& McIntyre, 1991), and Roy Miki for his essay on it,
"'Inside the Black Egg': Cultural Practice, Citizenship,
and Belonging in a Globalizing Canadian Nation,"
Mosaic 38.3 (2005): 1–19.

29.   "totalitarianism has discovered ...": This is from Hannah
Arendt, *The Origins of Totalitarianism*. New York:
Harcourt, 1976.

57.   "Raw or cooked": Grateful acknowledgment to jam
ismail and Roy Miki for a conversation about food and
Claude Lévi-Strauss, August 27, 2019.

58.   "Dear Echo": Many thanks to Dina Al-Kassim for her
work on Gayatri Spivak and Echo in "Listing Waters,"
in *Restorying Land: Canadian Literatures, Justice,
Relations*, forthcoming in fall 2021 from Wilfrid Laurier
University Press.

"Gardens are thus ...": This is from Monika Kin
Gagnon, "Tender Research: Field Notes from the

Nikkei Internment Memorial Centre, New Denver, BC," *Canadian Journal of Communication* 31.1 (2006): 215–225.

"Perhaps when we were raping ...": Diary of Azuma Shiro, a soldier during the Rape of Nanking, nagaikazu.la.coocan.jp/nanking/PART1_2.html#TOP, accessed June 1, 2018.

61. "Stretches animal skin over branches horns attached": Stephen Karcher, *Total I Ching: Myths for Change.* London: Time Warner, 2003.

Acknowledgments

This book was born in the midst of a great deal of cultural and political upheaval here in Canada and in Hong Kong, where my family is from. I am grateful to those who saw possibility in the whirling language early on. Dina Al-Kassim arranged an early performance of part of the work through the Critical Nationalisms, Counterpublics series at the Green College, UBC. Many kind supporters attended, but I remember especially the ever-supportive Strathcona crew, many of them my teachers, mentors and friends, including: Fred Wah, Pauline Butling, Meredith Quartermain, Peter Quartermain, Daphne Marlatt and Bridget MacKenzie. I would not be able to do any of this work without my chosen sisters, Hiromi Goto, Dana Putnam and Rita Wong, who were also there that day. The ever-supportive Smaro Kamboureli encouraged Nelson Wiseman to invite me to present another part of the work at the conference Permanently under Construction at the University of Toronto in 2017, which he generously did. Allie McFarland and Jordan Bolay published a few of the fragments in the first issue of their journal *Antilang*. I am grateful to Monika Kin Gagnon, whose "How to Banish Fear: Letters from Calgary" first showed me the power of epistolary in the early 1990s. We travelled together to Los Angeles to do a workshop with Deena Metzger in the summer of 2018, and it was through Deena's generous teaching that I learned that the I Ching is a turtle oracle. I am grateful for the invaluable conversations with Roy Miki and jam ismail over the years, especially recent(ish) ones at Honjin Yaletown Sushi Restaurant near Roundhouse Station in Vancouver. I am truly appreciative of my long-standing friendship with Nadine Chambers since the earliest days of my writing life and our ongoing conversation about Black/Asian/Indigenous relations, gender, queerness, power and how to live with and through institutions that sometimes support us and sometimes don't. Many thanks to Robert Majzels for intense conversations about Artaud's curses. Huge gratitude to Lillian Allen for her friendship, trust and gentle teaching. In Calgary, more friends, colleagues and students (some visiting and some long-term inhabitants) than I can name in this short text have been so supportive and wonderful, especially: Weyman Chan, Aruna Srivastava, Sharanpal Ruprai, Suzette Mayr, Nikki Sheppy, Shannon Maguire, Ian Williams, Liz Howard, Vivek Shraya, Rain Prud'homme-Cranford, Shaobo Xie, Nikki Reimer, Joshua Whitehead, Rebecca Geleyn, Mikka Jacobsen, Mahmoud Ababneh, Shuyin Yu, Trynne Delaney, Neil Surkan, Marc Lynch, Kaitlyn Purcell, Paul Meunier, Kathy Pham, Adrienne Rovere, Amy LeBlanc, Marjorie Rugunda, Ryan Sterne, Ben Groh, Colin Martin and Tom Sewel. Thank you to the Faculty of Arts and the English Department at the University of Calgary, and the Canada Research Chairs Program (SSHRC) for supporting this work.

Deep thanks to Brian Lam for publishing me again and for his ongoing belief in my work. Appreciation to Robert Ballantyne, working modestly behind the scenes, and especially for taking care of academic sales, as so many of my readers work in institutions. Heartfelt appreciation to Erín Moure, who edited the book and got me thinking about how spirits are at work in capitalization and punctuation, and talked me through difficult issues in both the writing and the sociality of poetry. Gratitude to her also for the turtle drawing that appears on the last page. This book would not be what it is without the generous, intelligent and full-hearted thoughts of Trish Salah, who was the book's "poethics" reader. Shirarose Wilensky came to the project as copy editor, but she has been so much more than that for this book, as she was in the editing of *The Tiger Flu*. I am grateful to her for her smart and open reading abilities, her eagle-sharp eyes and her ability and willingness to roll with a slightly kooky project. She has surely earned a special place in the cycles of rebirth for taking on this "copy editor's nightmare" with such grace and intelligence. Gratitude to Jazmin Welch for her incredible design work on the book, inside and out. Many thanks to Cynara Geissler and Jaiden Dembo for the hard work of publicity.

Finally, gratitude to my parents, Tyrone Lai and Yuen-Ting Lai, for sharing their stories with me and being okay with the complicated ways I carry history. Thank you to my sister, Wendy Lai, and her partner, Karel Maršálek, for supporting the work.

Love and appreciation to Edward Parker for trying his pedantic best to keep me in proper grammar.

Iron Goddess thanks the peopled palimpsest that composes her, some with apology, some with disdain, some with chagrin and some with great gratitude:

Bing Crosby, Thompson Twins, Andy Warhol, W.B. Yeats, Leonard Cohen, Michael Jackson, Wallace Stevens, Barbarella, Aqua, Djuna Barnes, William Shakespeare, J.R.R. Tolkien, Freddie Mercury, William Carlos Williams, The Normal, Bruce Cockburn, Fred Wah, bpNichol, Roy Miki, Mother Goose, Thomas Pynchon, Robert Graves, Walter Benjamin, Tim Hortons, The Beatles, Wolfgang Amadeus Mozart, jam ismail, Lewis Carroll, RuPaul, The Dead Milkmen, Thomas King, Ken Hughes, Jim Morrison, Sylvia Plath, Lu Xun, Iva Toguri, Idle Eyes, Thomas Dolby, Aretha Franklin, David Mamet, Alfred Hitchcock, Claude Lévi-Strauss, Robert Majzels, Michel Gondry and Charlie Kaufman, Iris Chang, Giacomo Puccini, the Bible, Ian Fleming, Jim Henson, Robert Louis Stevenson, Marie Clements, Nadine Chambers, Stanley Kubrick, Abba, Tina Turner, Pyotr Ilyich Tchaikovsky, Farrah Fawcett, Farid ud-Din Attar, Joshua Wong, The Carpenters, Mao Tse Tung, k-os, Wayson Choy, Boney M., Monopoly, Canadian Imperial Bank of Commerce, Kate Bush and any others who might have slipped through the cracks in her language.